8 Qualit
Success:
Leaders

The desert island challenge

Jeremy Sutcliffe

B L O O M S B U R Y

LONDON • NEW DELHI • NEW YORK • SYDNEY

Published 2013 by Bloomsbury Education
Bloomsbury Publishing plc
50 Bedford Square, London, WC1B 3DP

www.bloomsbury.com

978-1-4411-9750-4

A CIP record for this publication is available from the British Library.

1 3 5 7 9 10 8 6 4 2

Typeset by Fakenham Prepress Solutions, Fakenham, Norfolk, NR21 8NN
Printed by CPI Group (UK) Ltd, Croydon, CR0 4YY

This book is produced using paper that is made from wood grown in managed,
sustainable forests. It is natural, renewable and recyclable. The logging and
manufacturing processes conform to the environmental regulations of the
country of origin.

To see our full range of titles visit www.bloomsbury.com

Contents

Acknowledgements

No matter how well-constructed, a building only becomes a school once it is filled with real children and teachers. So it is with this book. Without the many passionate and dedicated school leaders who contributed it would be a hollow shell. Their wisdom, insights, real-life experiences and stories are what, I hope, will bring these pages to life for the reader. This book is dedicated to them.

First and foremost I would like to thank those who took part in my desert island challenge. Their thoughtful, fascinating and often inspiring contributions form the backbone of the book and many of these are reproduced in full, with their kind permission, in Appendix 1 (see page 148). Many of these successful leaders also agreed to be interviewed for the book and I am grateful to all of them for giving so generously of their time. They all deserve a name check here, so many thanks to: Geoff Barton, Headteacher, King Edward VI High School, Bury St Edmunds, Suffolk; Llyn Codling, Executive Headteacher, Portswood and St Mary's Church of England primary schools, Southampton; Andrew Fleck, Headmaster, Sedbergh School, Cumbria; Kenny Frederick, Principal, George Green's School, Tower Hamlets; Richard Harman, Headmaster, Uppingham School, Rutland; Russell Hinton, Headteacher, The Brier School, Kingswinford, Dudley; Andrew Hutchinson, Executive Principal, Parkside Federation Academies, Cambridge; Mike Kent, former Headteacher, Comber Grove Primary School, Camberwell, London; Dr John H. Newton, Headmaster, Taunton School, Somerset; Catherine Paine, Executive Headteacher, Mount Street Academy and Saxilby Church of England Primary School, Lincolnshire, N.B. Since being interviewed Catherine has taken up a new post as Assistant Chief Executive of REAch2 Academy Trust Waltham Forest London. Hamid Patel, Principal and Chief Executive, Tauheedul Islam Girls' High School, Blackburn; Roget Pope, Principal, Kingsbridge Community College, Devon; Derek Pringle, Headmaster, St George's College, Quilmes,

Buenos Aires, Argentina; Nigel Richardson, former Headteacher, The Perse School, Cambridge; Lynn Slinger, Headteacher, Forest Way Special School, Coalville, Leicestershire; Paul Smith, Principal, Parbold Douglas Church of England Academy, near Wigan, Lancashire; Bernard Trafford, Headmaster, Royal Grammar School, Newcastle; Teresa Tunnadine CBE, Headteacher, The Compton School, Finchley, London; Madeleine Vigar, Principal, The Castle Partnership Academy Trust, Haverhill, Suffolk.

Secondly, I would like to thank the following leaders for agreeing to be interviewed and sharing their insights: Maggie Farrar, former Executive Director and Interim Chief Executive, National College for School Leadership; Devon Hanson, Principal, Evelyn Grace Academy, Southwark; Sue Hargadon, Principal, Farlingaye High School, Suffolk; Dame Joan McVittie, Headteacher, Woodside High School, Wood Green, London; Ani Magill, Headteacher, St John the Baptist School, Woking, Surrey; Alison Peacock, Headteacher, The Wroxham School, Potters Bar, Hertfordshire; Patricia Scott, Headteacher, St Luke's High School, Barrhead, East Renfrewshire, Scotland; Nicola Shipman, Executive Headteacher, Fox Hill, Mansel and Monteney Primary Schools, Sheffield.

Thirdly, I would like to thank the following for their advice, helpful suggestions and guidance during the book's early planning stages: Sir Michael Barber, Chief Education Advisor, Pearson; Andy Buck, Managing Director of Academies, United Learning; Alan Hall, former Headteacher, Immanuel Church of England Community College and Belle Vue Girls' School, Bradford (my old English teacher); Geoff Lucas, former Secretary, Headmasters' and Headmistresses' Conference; Dr Sue Robinson; former Headteacher, Cherry Orchard Primary School, Birmingham; Huw Thomas, former Headteacher, Emmaus Catholic and Church of England Primary School, Sheffield and now Sheffield Diocesan Director of Education.

Having been a working journalist for 35 years (most of it covering education), I have a keen appreciation for the work of editors and am deeply grateful for the help and guidance of Holly Gardner, Anna Fleming, Jane Morgan and David Avital at Bloomsbury for helping to shape and give structure to what began as a half-formed idea composed in an e-mail when I had nothing better to do. Without their efforts the book would not be anything like as accessible as a resource to teachers and school leaders.

Finally, I would like to thank Sue Sutcliffe, my wife and partner in life, who encouraged me to write the book in the first place and greatly helped me with the whole project. Having finished the book, she will no longer be able to compare me to Edward Casaubon in George Eliot's *Middlemarch*. Mark!

Introduction: The desert island challenge

Eight key qualities to survive and prosper in school leadership.

What are the qualities needed to be a successful school leader? This is the question that this book sets out to answer. In my quest to find some answers one thing was clear right from the start. There is no simple formula that produces greatness in a headteacher or school principal. The best ones are individuals who know their own minds and have their own ideas. Yes, they are keen to learn from others about what works well elsewhere. They are also curious and enthusiastic about applying great ideas that they think will benefit their own pupils and staff. But they are their own men and women and they certainly are not clones.

So this is not a book that seeks to write a particular prescription for headship. It is not about government-led initiatives, top-down models or politically-directed attempts to change the culture of leadership in our schools. Instead it focuses on the vital ingredients and instincts that successful school leaders say have worked for them. As such, it attempts to sketch a portrait of modern headship, drawn from life. Around 30 school leaders contributed to the book, including more than 20 who agreed to be interviewed. Some work in highly disadvantaged primary and secondary schools while others are in prestigious schools in the independent sector. Many, but not all, are officially recognised as outstanding or excellent leaders by school inspectors and all of them are highly experienced and respected leaders in their profession.

The art and craft of headship

In contrast to many officially-approved publications this book does not attempt to identify 20 or 30 schools that meet fixed criteria for excellence. Nor does it attempt to do the same for the many excellent and splendid school leaders it features. It is not a book driven or determined by school performance data in any shape or form. Rather, it attempts to depict the real art and craft of headship by listening to a variety of very successful leaders working in a variety of different schools and settings. It is these leaders, not me, who have shaped this book and their insights and sound wisdom that – I hope – will provide a source of inspiration to all school leaders and anyone thinking about moving into headship.

In attempting to identify the key qualities most valued by successful leaders I began by talking to some headteachers I knew well. Some of these – including Kenny Frederick, Mike Kent, Geoff Barton and Roger Pope – feature prominently in these pages and I am grateful to all of them for helping to shape my approach. I was determined from the outset not to write a dry book about professional attributes and characteristics but one that would spark some lively discussions about the importance of headship and the kind of people we would like our school leaders – now and in future – to be.

Desert island challenge

My next step was to issue a challenge. To make it interesting I made it a kind of parlour game, based on the long-running BBC Radio Four programme *Desert Island Discs*. I invited school leaders to imagine they were cast adrift on a desert island with a school full of children in desperate need of a great headteacher. I asked them to consider what eight qualities they would take with them to run their desert island school. I was greatly helped by Maggie Farrar, then Executive Director at the National College for School Leadership, who kindly agreed to relay my challenge to headteachers and principals in the college's National Leaders of Education network. I am also grateful to Geoff Lucas, formerly Secretary of the Headmasters and Headmistresses' Conference (HMC) who generously offered to publish it in the association's newsletter. This brought correspondence from some surprising places, including from heads of international schools as far away as India and Argentina.

The response overall was a positive treasure trove of thoughtful contributions from some very impressive leaders. Their comments and insights form the backbone of this work and many of their contributions are reproduced at the back of this book (Appendix 1, see page 148). From their replies I began to see some common threads which could be woven into a narrative. But what also struck me was the many different qualities that are required – or at least desirable – to run a successful school. I found this reassuring as well as fascinating, especially the varying weight given to particular qualities by different leaders. It confirmed my belief that, while there might well be a common set of qualities which leaders agree are important and necessary, there is also scope for many different and distinctive styles of leadership.

What does it take?

Among the qualities most commonly identified by leaders are the need for:

- optimism
- calmness
- patience
- humility
- honesty
- trust.

Successful school leaders also need to be good team-builders who empower their staff and develop them to their full potential. They must be good organisers and pay attention to small details as well as being able to see the big picture. They also need a clear sense of moral purpose and to be highly visible role-models to their pupils and staff.

The ability to listen and be responsive to other people's needs and opinions is seen as a particularly important quality. Hamid Patel, Principal and Chief Executive of Tauheedul Islam Girls' High School in Blackburn, puts it this way:

"Outstanding leaders invite dissent and are prepared to listen to the views of others. They distribute leadership of responsibilities and create ownership of a problem rather than hand out a list of tasks for their subjects to complete. They are prepared to listen to the complaints of their staff and show that they are responsive to them. They also invite reasoned dissent from our young people, develop them to complain in a measured and constructive manner, and then show a willingness to respond to this. The days of the absolute leader, who decided and does everything, have gone a long time ago."

Another common thread is the importance of humour in school leadership. Paul Smith, Principal of Parbold Douglas Church of England Academy, a large village primary school in Lancashire, says the ability to share a joke can be invaluable "when we find ourselves up to our ears in the trenches".

"A sense of humour helps to develop team spirit and get people on side with you even if at times it is a delirious, or gallows humour. We have to remember that we are responsible for setting the mood and the ethos for the school. The best headteachers can turn some of the direst circumstances into positives or points for future development. It's amazing how a bit of blue sky thinking and talking can turn the gloomiest day around," he says.

Russell Hinton, Headteacher of The Brier School in Dudley, which caters for children with special educational needs, speaks for many when he identifies as a key quality: "Understanding that you are dealing with the most precious of things – people's children and all the hopes and dreams tied in with that."

One of the most thoughtful responses to my desert island challenge came from Bernard Trafford, Headmaster of the Royal Grammar School, in Newcastle. In particular, he speaks of some qualities being subsets of larger ones. Here is one of his desert island picks:

"Top comes courage for me, because if you don't have that you can't keep on course and drive through the things that need doing when things get tough. Nor can you be open, consultative and approachable, because asking people what they think doesn't always produce the answers or type of response you'd like! Determination is a subset of courage, as is confidence."

This helped to make it clear to me that the principal qualities required to be successful in school leadership depend, in turn, on a subset of related qualities and skills. Some of these are instinctive and some can be learned; some are innate while others are developed through experience. I now began to see both a structure to my book – with a chapter for each key quality (as I had always intended) – and a narrative for each major theme.

Influence of the National College

Two other influences came to bear on me in determining what those eight major themes should be. The first was the list of attributes and professional characteristics drawn up by the National College for School Leadership for the National Professional Qualification for Headship (NPQH) programme in 2011. The list outlines nine characteristics "shown by outstanding leaders" and includes many of the key words already mentioned in this introduction. It draws on extensive research as well as the *Outstanding Schools* series published by Ofsted, the school inspection service for England, in 2009 and 2010. These professional characteristics are reproduced at the end of this book (Appendix 2, see page 167).

I was also influenced by a short but invaluable paperback by Andy Buck, *What Makes a Great School?* (National College for School Leadership and the City Challenge Programme, 2009). This sets out a practical formula for successful leadership by Buck, a highly experienced former headteacher who is now Managing Director of Academies at United Learning, one of England's largest multi-academy providers. It includes chapters on leadership which focus on the 'behaviours and qualities' displayed by the best school leaders. In particular, it emphasises the importance of courage and communication, two aspects of leadership that feature prominently in this book.

Having decided on the key themes of the book my next task was to put some flesh on the bones. I wanted it to be a real conversation and a debate with and between leaders of the profession. I wanted to gently probe them for their views and tips and find out not just what it takes to run a successful school but what it actually feels like, deep down. I could only do that by talking directly to leaders. Many of those I spoke to took part in my desert island challenge. Others are leaders I already knew or who were recommended to me.

I also spoke at length to Maggie Farrar at the National College and her insights make an important contribution to the book. I will include two of them here. Firstly, when asked whether headship can be taught, she replied:

"Yes definitely. I am not one who believes that great leaders are born. Leaders are made from a combination of the leaders they meet, particularly if they are led by leaders who are outstanding. They learn by watching. They learn by being given opportunities to demonstrate and practise leadership on the job. They can also learn through formal leadership development provision, particularly when those programmes are rooted in the day-to-day realities of leadership and the leadership curriculum draws on the challenges and issues they face in their day-to-day work. Leadership can be taught. It requires an individual to be skilled at self-reflection because that is how you grow into being a leader. I don't think it can be taught in a lecture room and I don't think it can be learned through books. I think it's learned through doing."

The second insight came when I asked her whether there was a danger of the College, a government agency, imposing a leadership theology on the teaching profession and thereby stifling talent. This is what she said:

"No I don't. When we were redesigning the National Professional Qualification for Headship we had a group of 20 leaders working with us. One of the things they were really clear about is that the NPQH should not create clones. There must be room for the mavericks, the personalities, people who are very individual. There must be room for those traits and strong personalities to flourish and not feel they have to turn themselves into something they are not in order to be a headteacher."

Since our conversation took place two important changes have occurred concerning the government's relationship with school leadership development in England. The NPQH is now no longer a requirement for people taking up headships, raising the possibility that future leaders could be recruited from outside the profession. And in April 2013, the College was merged with the Teaching Agency and the new agency, the National College for Teaching and Leadership, will focus on school-based training and leadership development. Many of the leaders featured in this book will play a part in that development work. After serving as Interim Chief Executive of the National College for School Leadership in the run-up to the merger with the Teacher Training Agency, Maggie Farrar left the organisation in July 2013.

But while present and future governments will continue, for good or ill, to play a role in preparing leaders for headship, it is the profession itself that will continue to create the climate in which they operate. The qualities displayed by school leaders will shape the world in which generations of children will learn and grow up, both today and in the future. This book is about some of those remarkable leaders and the equally remarkable qualities that have contributed to their success.

1
Vision

> **Successful school leaders are visionaries with a clear sense of moral purpose. They can see and shape the future.**

If ever a school leader was shaped by his upbringing it is Devon Hanson. Born in Jamaica, he came to Britain at the age of nine and grew up on a council estate in Peckham, South London. Leaving school at 16, with few qualifications, he nevertheless showed his early ambition by securing a job in the City where he worked as a stockbroker for seven years. Then, in his mid-twenties, he decided to switch careers and become a teacher instead.

One of the seminal moments in his life came when he was sitting in an examination hall at South Thames College in Wandsworth, one of 150 applicants applying for 15 places reserved for mature students on a teaching degree course at Roehampton College.

> "I looked at the paper and thought, 'Oh no, I can't do this, it's too difficult'. As I got onto my feet to leave I noticed four or five others doing the same and they were all black people. There weren't that many in there in the first place. So I thought, 'You had better sit down, it looks bad you walking out'. So I sat down, read the questions again and then I just started to write. That was on a Tuesday and to my surprise on the Wednesday morning my lecturer rang me up, excited and said they wanted to interview me. She said they thought my papers were amazing. I went for an interview on the Friday and they said within hours they would like me on the course."

Inner city learning

The knowledge that he almost walked away from that challenge has stayed with him for a quarter of a century. It was the opportunity that put him on the road to a successful career in a profession he loves. By staying the course and gaining a Bachelor of Education (B.Ed.) degree at Roehampton he soon found himself back in the neighbourhood he grew up in, this time teaching children just like himself. It is a situation he clearly relishes. A natural story-teller who obviously feels a deep affinity for disadvantaged children, he went on to build his career as a pastoral leader and trouble-shooter in challenging secondary schools in Lambeth and Southwark.

In 2007, he was offered his first headship as Principal of Walworth Academy in Southwark, one of the first academies in London and a flagship project for the sponsor, ARK Schools, now one of the country's biggest academy chains. The new academy was replacing Walworth School which had been placed in special measures by the school inspection service, Ofsted. It was a tough assignment, especially for a first-time head, and Hanson admits he was apprehensive to begin with because Walworth School had a long-standing reputation for racial intolerance. Many local black and Asian parents preferred to send their children to other schools in the area. Nevertheless he accepted the challenge.

"I went through a lot of soul-searching as to how I was going to project myself. I decided that my stance and my ethos would be, 'We are one, we work together'."

Equal opportunities for all

In Hanson's view, you have to have a sense of purpose in order to be a successful school leader. For him, it is not just a matter of drawing up a mission statement or a business plan. It has to come from within. In his own case, that inner belief comes from a career of teaching in inner-city schools which has given him the deep conviction that all children should be given the same opportunities to succeed. It was this vision that he set out to achieve at Walworth Academy.

"I had to sit back and think, 'What do I stand for? Am I just there to teach the children ABC123, or is there something bigger than that?' My vision is bigger than that. There's a social context that I have to take on board. My vision was to create a community within the school that supports each other no matter where you're coming from, boy or girl. It doesn't matter about your gender. I was going to 'live equal opportunities', in every way, in every shape and in everything we do in the academy.

"When I first came to Walworth the staff told me there was this big debating competition going on and I said, 'Yes, we should enter the children'. And they picked the five brightest children that they thought they had in the school. When they called their names to me I said, 'No, they're not the best people' and they said 'Yes, they are the brightest children', and I said 'No they're not'. I didn't know these children but I recognised the names were all of African descent. I had to say to them, 'All those names are of black children aren't they?' They said yes, they were, and I said: 'That is not what we will represent. That is not a true representation of the academy and I would rather have a true representation.'

"It was important for me to have that. It was important for parents and the children to see that we were all together. I wanted the groups from Bermondsey and the groups from Peckham and Walworth to see that. If you look at our prospectuses and all our communications with parents, on no one page would you see one single nation. You always see the diversity of what we are and to me that was important. So my vision was, and is, to shape the social context as well as the academic side of things. You have to have a vision, you have to set your mind on it and you have to say 'Right, now I'm going to work with it regardless'. I will help people, support people to come along with me. I can't do it alone. It's the skill of knowing how to bring others with you, to share that vision, to make the vision clear and to say 'Yes, I can buy into that'."

Under new management

It is easy to dismiss the concept of 'vision' as something that is vague and woolly. This is understandable given the many examples of school 'vision statements' that are bland and meaningless and often quietly discarded after the first flush of enthusiasm. Many teachers and school leaders regard such statements as little more than a marketing tool, a way of rebranding a school when a new head comes in and a convenient way of announcing it is 'Under new management'. Geoff Barton, Headteacher of King Edward VI School, a popular community comprehensive in Bury St Edmunds, Suffolk, takes a typically sceptical view.

> "I am a bit sniffy about the word 'vision' actually having done my NPQH headship qualification twice. I failed it the first time because I didn't write it up in the appropriate format, which is a bit of a badge of honour for me. They just talked endlessly about vision and values and I think in some ways they overstate it because in the job you never lie awake thinking, 'What is my vision?' You are much more likely to lie awake thinking about a conversation with an NUT rep the next morning, and I think maybe more time should be put into that. So I cringe a little bit when I hear myself talking about vision. It's more important for me to ask, 'What do we want a really good school to be?' The answer is that we want to be as good as we can inside the classroom and as good as we can outside the classroom."

Principles and values

Underpinning Barton's scepticism however is a clear sense of purpose that is firmly rooted in the practicalities of running a mixed-ability school in an English provincial town. What is distinctive about the school is that it is an outward-looking community school that is actively engaged with the population it serves and constantly on the look-out for opportunities and making connections that will benefits its pupils.

> "I've sat through so many sessions where everybody has to present their vision of what a great school is going to be and essentially they say the same thing. They say, 'We want children to be happy, we want them to be successful; we want teachers to be happy, we want them to be successful'. I mean, what is there to argue against really? It should be taken as read. I don't think that that is necessarily a vision. I think the language I would use is about principles and values. What do I believe in? What do I want a youngster – whether they are from a children's home or from a very privileged background – what would I like that youngster to have experienced? What would I like them to be able to do? How can we as a school help to do that for them? That seems to me a more interesting concept because it leads you into what is distinctive about your own school and that's where I think we are very clear about what we are trying to do and what is distinctive and what is rubbish and what we shouldn't do.

"There are some schools, I think deplorably, that have changed their curriculum in order to boost their performance table position. We would never do that. We would introduce courses because we have children for whom those courses are appropriate. We resisted doing many vocational courses for example, even though they would obviously have moved us up the performance tables and if you look at our data you would think it was an underperforming school because it's being judged against schools that are packing GCSE equivalents into every student's lunchbox. We would never ever do that and the governors are very strong on that.

"I think that is one of the distinctive features; that we keep trying to do things that matter for the youngsters that we have got and the parents we've got and we resist some of the nonsense that just gets you through hoops. That's what makes questionable some of the discussions people have about vision and values because those people are often the first to jump through government hoops."

From special measures to outstanding

One successful school leader noted for her independence – and not one to jump through hoops for the sake of it – is Alison Peacock, Headteacher of The Wroxham School in Potters Bar, Hertfordshire. Having taken over the primary school in 2003 when it was in special measures, it was transformed under her leadership and graded as 'outstanding' by Ofsted three years later. The school now has an international reputation for its creative curriculum and became a National Teaching School in 2011.

"When I went for my interview I was asked where the school would be in five years. The PowerPoint slide that I used at that interview is still on my wall. The first thing I said was I wanted the school to be a happy learning community, with high academic standards, achievement for all, partnership and learning, become a centre of excellence with a broad and balanced curriculum. That was the vision from day one."

While the use of a PowerPoint presentation may not sound especially visionary, Peacock's approach to her first headship was strongly based on principles drawn from best practice. She had been involved in a research project called *Learning Without Limits*, published by Open University Press in 2004. Her own teaching practice had been studied as part of the research.

"Because of that I had a greater clarity about what it was that I was seeking to do. My own practice had been researched and we'd had feedback. That level of research within the research community I think has been a really powerful influence on my leadership," she says.

Climate of trust

Her vision for where she wanted to take her school was founded on a carefully worked out programme.

"It is very strongly led by a set of principles which are about the notion that inclusion is vital for everybody, children and adults. There's a sense that we need to develop a climate of trust rather than a climate of fear, so that the children can trust the teachers and the teachers can trust the children, and that parents and everybody on the staff trust each other. That notion of trust is really key. And also the notion of co-agency, the notion that together we can create something that we wouldn't be able to do on our own and that's about sharing ideas and a confident dialogue of debate between children and the staff and between children and the community, in order that we can constantly improve what we are about. Those are the underpinning principles.

"When I started, the school had been in special measures and the teachers were exhausted and the children were de-motivated. Everybody was in a kind of environment where there was a sense that you just had stuff done to you. The teachers felt that they were being monitored and judged and that someone was going to tell them what they needed to do in order to improve. Similarly the children were in a position where their behaviour had to be sorted out because Ofsted had described the children as being un-teachable. So quite often they were passive in the classroom and quite aggressive on the playground.

"As a new head I felt I wanted to reawaken the sense of purpose and the notion that learning is transformative. So we brought in people to work alongside the staff and the children. Instead of just judging the teaching they came in and taught. They might be artists, or musicians or poets. We also had a teenage rock band. They came in and lifted the aspirations of everybody. Often when children work with someone with a passion and an expertise in a particular area they shine in a way they hadn't realised they might be able to. It's great for the children and for the teachers watching them."

A crucial part of realising her vision was winning the support of the staff and she took instant steps to bring this about.

> "Before I even took up the post I asked for the interim head to arrange a time when I could meet with every individual teacher for an hour to talk to them and listen to them about what they thought was important. I asked each of them, 'How could we make things better for you?' So instead of a deficit model which said, 'I've read the reports on you and you need to improve on X, Y and Z,' it was very much more, 'Tell me how it feels to be working in the school at the moment and what is it that needs to happen to enable you to feel more confident'. Very often they were very practical things, like the Foundation Stage teacher who said to me, 'They keep on telling me that I need to do more outdoor learning but we haven't got a fence so the children run away'.
>
> "The other thing that really astounded me was when someone said to me, months later: 'You were the first person to ask us what we thought'. So the school had gone into an Ofsted category and nobody had asked the teachers what they felt would make a difference, or at least that was what the teachers felt. There was an assumption that someone was going to come in and do it to you. That's hugely disempowering and makes you feel that you haven't got any of the answers so why try and seek them because someone else is better than you. As soon as you get into that mind-set everything is going to feel far more difficult than it needs to."

Tough assignment

Another leader who believes you need a clear vision to run a school success-fully is Dame Joan McVittie, Headteacher of Woodside High School in Wood Green, North London.

"You have to know what an excellent school looks like in order to take the school there. You just cannot afford to be wishy-washy around that," she says.

In 2005, McVittie was asked by Haringey council to take over at what was then called White Hart Lane School, just down the road from Tottenham Hotspur's football club, which was in special measures. At the time she was head of Leytonstone School in North-east London and working as a consultant leader for London Challenge, an ambitious school improvement programme which began in 2003 under the direction of the then Commissioner for London Schools, Sir Tim Brighouse. She had been looking for a new headship, preferably a tough assignment where she felt she could make a difference. Her description of her first visit to the school gives an indication of what she was taking on.

"There was total chaos on the corridors. The children were on the corridors all the time, even beyond the change of lessons. When they should have been really involved in their work they were on the corridors wandering. There were pockets of excellent teaching but they were few and far between. People talked behind closed doors. It was a real badge of honour to say, 'We work in the worst school in London, aren't we wonderful?'"

A personal vision

McVittie has a reputation as an inspirational but also practical leader. For her, the vision is a personal one. At White Hart Lane she set about creating a school that could offer its pupils the same opportunities for learning and success that she wanted for her own children.

> "The key thing was first and foremost to provide a climate for learning where the children felt safe so that we could raise attainment. The end point has to be raised attainment. I'm a parent myself and for me the key thing is the school should be educating a child and giving them a passport to success in later life. That passport takes the form, first and foremost, of examination results otherwise you don't even get an interview. And secondly it's about developing a rounded child, one that can speak up and do things and think about others.
>
> "The school has got a two-pronged attack. The key one is attainment. What I always say is I sent my own daughters to school to get a good clutch of GCSEs and A-levels. It would be very nice if the school could turn them into civil human beings at the same time but if they don't I'll have a good go at doing that myself. So the key one really was attainment and everything was about creating the right climate to raise attainment."

The importance of attainment

This emphasis on the importance of attainment is particularly striking among leaders in inner-city schools. For headteachers like Joan McVittie and Devon Hanson examination success offers their pupils a golden ticket to a better future. Theirs is very often a personal vision, a powerful sense of purpose or calling that shapes their approach to headship. Many leaders refer to this as 'moral purpose', a determination to shape young people's futures for the better. While there are undoubtedly some school leaders who achieve success by manipulating their intake and focusing ruthlessly on league tables, the best leaders put the needs of their pupils and parents before the interests of the school. McVittie's vision for her school is to continue making improvements for the benefit of local children, despite a huge rise in attainment and an 'outstanding' grading from Ofsted.

"We've still got a way to go. I want to keep pushing up those exam results and we still have the same intake we had in 2005. I haven't altered my client base and got more middle-class children. I've still got the same children from deprived backgrounds. To be recognised as outstanding by Ofsted is good but I want grade ones across the board. We know the areas where we need to do extra work. I don't think any headteacher is ever finished. There are always some areas for improvement."

Improving a successful school

Uppingham School in rural Rutland is one of Britain's best known and grandest public schools and could not be more different from Woodside High School. When Richard Harman was appointed Headmaster there in 2006 he faced a very different situation to the one McVittie had to deal with.

"It was a very successful school, well run with a good name. That was the challenge in a way, taking it from what was already a very high level to the next level."

Even so, the qualities required to run a successful school are largely universal, he believes. In order to succeed, school leaders must have a clear vision of where they want to take their organisation. He defines it as "the ability to formulate and shape the future, rather than be shaped by events". Developing a vision and being able to articulate it, he says, is crucial because everyone involved in the school – pupils, staff and parents – need to know where they are going.

"The Biblical line is, 'Where there is no vision the people perish' [Proverbs 29:18] and the opposite is also true. As long as it is a realistic and achievable vision – as well as highly aspirational – then people will follow. They need a direction. They need to know what the journey is. One also needs to weave in other people's views, but first and foremost you have to be able to articulate that journey so that they will follow. It's part of the challenge of leadership."

Unexpected events, ranging from the mundane to the dramatic, are a constant source of tension for any headteacher. They have the potential to derail or undermine the best-laid plans and the way a leader responds can make or break a headship. Harman quotes the words attributed to Harold Macmillan when he was asked what a prime minister feared most: 'Events, dear boy, events'. It is exactly the same for headteachers, Harman says.

"Events can always take you off track from your plan. You have to be a tactician, able to respond to events. On the other hand if you are not careful you could spend your whole day just being reactive, or even your whole career, because there is so much to react to. You need to be able to see the wood for the trees, even whilst you are dealing with the reaction. So being able to keep your vision clear and articulate it even in the midst of some major event or sequence of events is really important."

A passion for learning

Respect for the individual and nurturing a passion for learning lie at the centre of Harman's vision for Uppingham School.

"At the core is a passionate belief in the sacredness of education. Someone [the philosopher Michael Oakeshott] once said that education was a conversation between the generations. Creating and nurturing the spaces for those conversations, especially under the pressures of league tables and results, is vital. The sanctity of the individual and the strong belief that we are not just dealing with numbers in a league table or a process as in a sausage factory, but we are actually dealing with unique individuals, all of which have a God-given talent: that is a great calling. The vision for school leaders is the out-working of that: what that means in terms of being able to provide the right opportunities and the right people to support each child and be able to provide the opportunities for transformation. That is a very great privilege. That's at the core of the vision. One can talk about building plans and master plans but those are the out-working of the vision rather than the end in itself."

Capturing enthusiasm

In a very different context comes the view of Mike Kent, one of the country's longest-serving headteachers, until his recent retirement after 31 years at the helm at Comber Grove Primary School in Camberwell, South London. He also believes a clear vision, founded on a passionate commitment to the joy of learning, is essential to run a successful school.

"I think that primary education should be a voyage of discovery. Children should be able to come into a school and be able to experience a vast range of things. It's absolutely not about getting children to jump through hoops. Yes, children have to be able to write, they have to be able to read and add up. But more than that, primary education is so important for social intercourse, teaching children to get on with each other and be tolerant. It's about all the things they need to experience: drama, music, art, reading, writing and all the things that go on after school. I run a film club, there's a jazz club, all sorts of games activity. Children should wake up in the morning and think, 'I want to get to school today because I want to finish that model,' or 'I want to finish that story'. They should love primary education and really want to go to school. If you can capture their enthusiasm for learning and knowledge in the primary years then you are well on your way. We get lovely reports from our secondary schools because they say our children are interesting, they are well behaved and enjoy learning. That is so important.

"What I've done at Comber Grove is gather a group of teachers who feel the same way about primary education. If you turn it into a cramming institution, which unfortunately so many so-called outstanding primary schools are, I think that is just so wrong. I think you are just putting children off education, not being inclusive."

"My vision is about children loving school and experiencing a vast range of things and having a group of teachers that thoroughly enjoy being with children. If you look at our classrooms they are full of artwork, full of models, there's always lots of things going on and that's as interesting for the teachers as it is for the children. You find the staff are very rarely away because they love coming to work. It's as simple as that. Similarly for me; I've never got up in the morning and felt I don't want to go to work because every day is so fascinating and every day is so different."

Fulfilling potential

Ani Magill, Headteacher of St John the Baptist, a high performing Catholic comprehensive in Woking, Surrey, says her vision for her school "is about ensuring students fulfil their potential". As head of the school since 1995, her longstanding aim has been to make the school the best in England, combining high academic achievement with an emphasis on developing students who are happy and well-rounded. But while she thinks it is important to have a vision of where you want to take your school as a leader she is nevertheless sceptical about the way the word is often misused.

> "Personally, I don't like the word vision because I've met heads before who have a vision but then, if people don't like that vision, then they get another one. Well that isn't a vision. Vision is something that you believe in deep down. At St John the Baptist we want our children to be happy and we want them to be successful in all ways, but overarching that we want three things. We want them to get better exam results than in any other school, however much money they charge. Secondly, because the children that are in school now are going to be living and working in the year 2080 we have got to prepare children for that. They are going to be doing jobs that haven't yet been invented. That's not just about knowledge and exams, it's about having all those soft skills that they will need: teamwork, communication skills and the flexibility to be able to do those jobs and adapt to changing times in the future. And the third thing is for us to try and show them by example so that they will go out and live good Christian lives. The values and the morals to know what it means to be an upstanding person in society and to treat people in the way that they would hope they would treat them."

A golden thread that connects successful leaders, even those who are sceptical about 'vision statements' and suspicious about so-called 'visionary' headteachers, is the belief that underlying everything they do is a deep sense of purpose and moral integrity, an inner belief that what they are attempting to achieve is right for their school and for their pupils. Magill likens it to having a moral compass and says that without it no school leader can be truly effective.

"You do see a lot of heads, usually men, who think being a headteacher is about having their own car parking space, having a school iPad and having a big name on their door and being able to bark orders to people. Although not so much nowadays, perhaps; I think attitudes are shifting."

A shared vision

One of the most important aspects of leadership is developing a shared vision about the direction a school needs to take. It is not enough to have conviction that you are doing the right thing. It is not enough to be able to articulate that vision clearly, although that is the crucial next step. In order to create the conditions to make it a reality you need to be able to share it with others. At St John the Baptist School the leadership team has developed a Ten-point model that provides "a no-nonsense explanation to what we consider to be the outstanding features of successful leadership". Each characteristic described begins with one of the letters in the word LEADERSHIP. The characteristic beginning with the letter 'S' is:

"Share your vision. AT SJB our vision is about ensuring students fulfil their potential. It is important that you explain what this means to your teams and explain the benefits of achieving this aim." (Appendix 3, see page 168).

Llyn Codling, Executive Headteacher of Portswood and St Mary's Church of England primary schools in Southampton, is another who believes a leader must develop a shared vision a take a school forward. One of the potential pitfalls of leadership is allowing yourself to be driven by your own ego, she says.

"It's about getting that aspect under control in your own mind. You are there to serve a community and therefore you need to get your own ego out of it and look at what is right for that community. What is right for that school? What has the previous head done that is already fantastic? Your job is to build upon that and don't have any of this nonsense of, 'Well, I've got to make myself look big and great', because actually you don't. You've got to keep the school going. For me it's about 'servant leadership'. It's about: 'What can I do when I'm caretaking this school?' 'What can I do to make the growth of the school be maintained and develop?' rather than, 'What can I do for the glory of me?'"

When Codling was appointed Headteacher of Portswood in 2006 it was already graded as 'outstanding' by Ofsted. Her task as the new head was to maintain the best features of the school while working with the staff and governors to develop a fresh vision for its future.

"I think it has to be a shared vision. I think as a leader you sometimes walk behind that vision and sometimes you hold that vision up but I do think it's a shared vision and I think that any leader who has no vision is not going anywhere."

Soon after taking up her headship at Portswood she held a staff training day to work on developing a shared vision.

"I remember it well because it was really scary and it was about developing a vision for the school. I called it, 'Blue Skies and Fluffy White Clouds' and I wanted people's ideas for where we were going, but I laid my own vision on the line very early on. I made clear what I was passionate about and what my beliefs were. My beliefs are about Quality First teaching, high Assessment for Learning and great leadership and those are the qualities that drive a school up. My question to them all was: 'So if we are outstanding, a) how do we maintain 'outstanding' and b) why are we not in the top 200?'"

The discussion with the staff clearly bore fruit. The following year, the school was again graded 'outstanding' by Ofsted. The inspection report noted: "The school's aim of developing pupils' 'Pride, passion and success' is fully met".

Hearts and minds

Catherine Paine is Executive Headteacher of Mount Street Academy, an infant and nursery school in Lincoln, and Saxilby Church of England Primary, a neighbouring village school just outside the city. She believes that in order to achieve success as a school leader you have to be able to win over "hearts and minds".

"What I mean by winning hearts and minds and inspiring other people is really about making sure that everybody you are working with and come into contact with has signed up to the vision you have for your school. For example as a National Leader of Education I have been working in a school that's been in an Ofsted category causing concern to the local authority. The difference it's made has been huge.

"On the first day of term in September, an Inset day, which was the first time I'd met the staff, we shared together a vision for the school around three words, 'Time to shine'. We commissioned a school song which says, 'Now is the time to shine' which spells out what that means: to be the very best version of yourself. We put it all over the website and the newsletters and we have a parents' assembly on a Friday which is just called Shine, where the children are there for their achievements, both inside and outside the school. It showcases gymnastics, literacy work and drama. The word 'shine' just seems to have transformed the school and the community's view of itself because in actual fact nothing on the first of September changed except that people began to believe in themselves again and to believe in their vision for the school.

"And because those three words go through everything we do, like the words through a stick of rock, everything is about the children's work being the best it can be. It's about teachers being on a career path that feels meaningful to them and they can see that CPD is leading them in a direction of greater leadership opportunities. It's about their careers shining. On parents' evenings it's about showing the parents how the children are shining in school. It's as though those three simple words have given people something deep inside themselves to feel inspired by."

Paine acknowledges the danger that this approach could be viewed as nothing more than an instant makeover unless parents and staff are fully on board. The important thing is to develop a vision that can win hearts and minds and be used as a sustainable programme of action for the school. The fact that she has achieved something similar at Mount Street, which became one of England's first primary school academies in October 2011, suggests the formula works.

"I have been here at Mount Street for nine years and we have a similar tag-line which is 'Creating a haven in which children flourish'. The words 'haven' and 'flourish' are concepts that everybody who works here under-stands and supports. Everyone, from cleaner to teaching assistant, would be able to authentically describe how they contribute towards the school being a haven and how they help children to flourish. And they would be really clear on exactly what their role is in living out that vision and in case anyone has forgotten we remind them every September when we do a big piece of work on Inset day around what those words mean for us when we induct new staff.

"Everything we do is around 'flourishing' and 'being a haven' for children. It's also about holding people to account, so if I hear a midday supervisor shouting at a child they are hauled into my office. There's no place for a raised voice in a haven. It's just not haven-like to shout. It can be both a carrot and a stick sometimes as well."

Having a plan

While it is essential to have a vision for a school there also has to be a plan to make it real, according to Maggie Farrar, former Executive Director of the National College for School Leadership.

"Everybody wants to know when they follow a leader what that leader stands for and what that leader believes in and the degree of ambition that leader has for the school, the staff, the community," she says.

"A leader must be able to articulate their vision – I would call it their aspiration – and be prepared to debate and discuss it with their staff and young people in their school. People are trying to get clues about that vision from a leader all the time or are working it out in other ways. What does this leader think is important, or not important? But there's no point in having a vision without a plan of how to achieve it."

Moral purpose

To Teresa Tunnadine, Headteacher at The Compton School in North London, having a sense of moral purpose is more important than the vision that stems from it.

"The vision is just the practicalities of what is the next stage. How do we translate improvement, how do we break it down, what are the specifics that we need to do next, whether it's focusing on IT, lesson observation, expanding or opening a sixth form? I think the vision is translating the moral purpose into something concrete."

For her, moral purpose "is absolutely about why I do this job, why I went into teaching and why I've gone into headship".

"It's about making a difference to children's lives and their life chances. I think your vision for what you need to do next comes out of that. You have to make sure that it's always about making things better for the children in your care and giving them a better deal. It's also about making sure you are giving yourself a good deal. It's about moral purpose for the staff too;

enabling them, encouraging and supporting them. So it's absolutely about moral purpose, about why we do what we do, working in the social service that we are. The vision comes out of that: 'What do I have to do to make things better here?'"

When Tunnadine moved to The Compton as a deputy head in 1992, it was a Fresh Start school, its predecessor having been shut down by the local authority. Under new leadership the school became very successful and went on to be graded 'outstanding' by Ofsted. When the headteacher left in 1999, Tunnadine was appointed to the top job. Under her leadership the school has grown substantially and is now massively oversubscribed.

As a long-standing headteacher she believes an important aspect of successful leadership is being able to inject new energy and purpose periodically into a school. It is about knowing when to instigate major change and then pursuing it single-mindedly.

"I am a firm believer in the Sigmoid Curve theory of leadership which is that the best time to change an organisation is when it is at its most successful. It's based on an S-shaped curve, which is on its side. When you get to the top of the hump, if you carry on doing what you are doing, you will slide back down the S. To get to the next peak, at the point of huge success where everything is going well you have to disconnect and do something completely different. Every five years in a school's life, I believe, you have to do something different just when you think things are fine and right and working. The temptation is to carry on, but we don't. We think right, let's have a new start.

"For example the first round of expansion at The Compton School kick-started us into working in a new way. We had another kick-start where we did 20 observations of lessons a week. At the time there were no lesson observations going on. This was when I first became a head and was something we decided we needed to do to really improve the quality of teaching and learning and to squeeze every last drop of learning out of the lesson.

"That caused massive improvement. It was a very detailed programme that took place over four or five years and improved every single aspect of teaching and learning. That was a vision that I had; that we needed to deconstruct the lessons and make sure that everybody was trained and had feedback to make sure that they were as good as they could be. I think having a vision is about knowing what your school needs and going for it single-mindedly and explaining to staff what we need to do and why we need to do it."

Telling stories

Roger Pope, Principal of Kingsbridge Community College in Devon, is another leader who recalls having to give a talk about his vision for his school as part of his NPQH course.

> "To me it was obvious what you want for the school. You want all children to achieve and you want equal opportunities and you want to be the best. Yet actually when you go into different schools you realise that people do have very different visions of what they want and you can feel those differences in their schools. I will stand up in front of the staff and will say, 'I want you to enjoy your work here'. I will tell them, 'I think we have a moral duty in what we do and therefore I want to involve you in decisions' and that our children must have high aspirations. I will articulate all that very clearly.
>
> "I'm also a great believer in telling stories. In our last three-year development plan we had a strategy that was called *One Hundred and Eighty!* And was the ultimate Eddie Bristow darts thing where we decided to aim for 100 per cent GCSE A*–C grades, including English and maths. We would tell a story around why we were doing that and why it was appropriate. You set out visions in terms of where you want the school to be and where you are aiming. In that sense they are a kind of shorter-term management planning, a sub-plot of the overall story."

Programme of action

It is this translation of moral purpose into a practical programme of action or the development of a particular ethos for a school that most leaders would recognise as 'vision'. That sense of purpose invariably stems from a set of core principles and beliefs which may be a strong commitment to social justice, to the sacredness of education, to developing the individual or simply having high expectations for every child.

What is striking is that while many of the most successful leaders are critical about the damaging impact of performance tables on schools and the quality of learning, none deny the importance of helping their pupils to obtain the qualifications they need to be successful. Having a sense of moral purpose is all very well but in the end it is results that really matter, for pupils as well as schools. Pope believes the two go hand-in-hand.

"The buzz phrase is moral purpose and I think that is really important. I think a lot of people would start from the point that they come into teaching because they like being with children and they like the interaction with children. I don't think many people come in because they want to make the world better by working with children, though I think that as you go up through headship then that is a powerful driver. But I think it would be naïve to somehow pretend that was completely separate from also needing to get exam results up and get high in the league tables and all the rest of it.

"Moral purpose is important but I think there are some schools for whom that becomes muddled so they somehow then say, 'We are about moral purpose, we're about children thriving and developing and that's more important than exam results'. I always say the two are inseparable, because if your purpose is to give children the best opportunity in life, how are you going to do that if they haven't got their GCSEs in maths and English?

"That's what gives them their passport for the future. Interestingly, I think schools have become much more moral places because over the last ten to fifteen years we have learned to care much more about children than perhaps we used to. I think there was a culture in the past where if kids succeeded and passed exams then, 'Great'. But if they didn't then, 'Let them truant and bunk off and we don't have to worry about them'."

What has changed, he believes, is that increased investment, combined with a greater emphasis on accountability has encouraged schools to focus on individual children, especially those struggling to achieve.

"The extra money that's flowed into schools has enabled them to employ teaching assistants, counsellors and lots of other things. The fact that we have been able to invest in that kind of service has made us think about what we are doing more. I think that is a factor. I think that interestingly what happens with the league tables is that if you are fighting to get 30 to 40 per cent GCSE A*–C grades, including English and maths, that's really important. Once you get up to 70 to 80 per cent then you suddenly become aware of the fact that unless you also actually seek to reward and include that other 20 per cent then they get an even worse deal because they feel more and more as if they haven't succeeded. So in a bizarre way it does drive you to think about these kids more. The increased emphasis on equal opportunities has certainly been a factor because it makes you think of all children."

2
Courage

Successful school leaders are courageous and determined, with the willpower and patience to see things through.

On 5th May, 2010, the *Daily Mail* newspaper carried a story under the following headline: 'The Uppingham Revolt: Public school pupils say they were RIGHT to stage mass mutiny over expelled schoolmates'.

It was a typical tabloid story, full of gleeful outrage that a 'mob' of pupils from 'an elite public school' should stage a 'mutiny over mass expulsions'. It likened the incident, which blew up after seven sixth-formers were expelled by headmaster Richard Harman for bullying a fellow student, to 'the notorious film *If...* in which a boarding school rises in violent rebellion against oppressive teachers'.

A difficult and unpleasant decision

The story, says Harman, was somewhat exaggerated but even so he remembers the occasion as one of the most difficult moments of his life.

"It was very difficult. Before I took that decision, there was a build-up and a background to it. One of the challenges was that there were multiple families involved. It was the perfect storm in that respect. In some senses you can't prepare for it, you just have to deal with it. I knew before I made my decision that it was going to be difficult and unpleasant, though I didn't know how difficult and unpleasant.

"Sometimes you have to withdraw and go into your own quiet space to reflect and that's what I did because I knew that potentially if this went really badly wrong my job would be on the line. Although all the stuff that was thrown at me in my view was unjustified you still have to deal with it and you still feel it. I had to be prepared so that when it came to it the underlying issues mattered sufficiently for me to take that risk, or to know that if the worst happened and my trustees didn't back me and I lost my job then I would have felt that I had done the right thing. It comes down to moral courage. It was one of those moments when I had to go into a quiet place and be at peace with the decision."

At stake was the school's whole approach to discipline and, more fundamentally, its core values about how people in a boarding school community should treat each other.

"The issue was bullying and also it touched on a culture of behaviour in a particular group in a particular house. It was a no-win situation whichever decision I made. It was going to be difficult or wrong for some people so I knew it was going to be hard either way. In the end it was about what kind of behaviour and what kind of values mattered most, whatever the ins and outs about what people felt about it. What would this say about the school in terms of the values I felt were most important? What is and isn't acceptable about the way we treat each other in a community living together? It's one of the most important questions that can face a headteacher. If you don't tackle those things in one place they will pop up in other places."

The benefits of making a stand

Although it was a difficult period, he believes the school has benefited from his uncompromising decision to make a stand.

"My perspective now is that although there will still be some people who feel bruised by it – and it was also a very difficult time for my family – the school as a community is definitely stronger. Every crisis is an opportunity and it was an opportunity to restate our core values and why they are so important; to say that this is the kind of community we are and to which we all belong. If there is one thing that I hate it's arrogance and of course that has been a besetting challenge for some public school pupils in the past.

"I said to the school that in the future arrogant public school pupils are not going to get the time of day from anybody. You have got to learn that and that having the right attitude in terms of behaviour towards other people, whether they are close by you or not is vital in life. So it was an opportunity to really restate those values.

"It was important also for the staff because it was an opportunity to actually draw them closer in with me as a whole team and they were fantastically supportive. There were moments when it was a bit of a siege mentality but out of that came a much stronger, closer bond because they'd seen me going through it; the resilience and moral courage had been shown, the vision was there and we came through it.

"I think they felt, although not always at the time, that we were much stronger as a result. There was an opportunity for team-building there as well and a real debate about what our values were. That also strengthened the culture. So there were a lot of positives to set against the negative feelings that some undoubtedly felt. There was vast support from the majority of parents, the community and alumni."

A career-defining moment

Harman was well aware that whatever decision he took could make or break his career.

"It was going to be a defining moment. I would not have chosen to go through that, but events happen. The important thing is to be able to deal with those events but also keep your values and your vision."

The incident forced him to draw deeply from the well of what he calls 'moral courage'. To headteachers like him who have to face up to difficult situations this is more than simply being determined. It is being determined about something that really matters. This form of courage is not only needed in exceptional circumstances. It is like a muscle and you have to be ready to exercise it from time to time to support your aspirations and values. Sometimes it is an automatic reflex to a routine event or problem.

Occasionally it calls for a Herculean effort in order to see things through. It is also about leading by example.

> "I don't think you have to be a tub-thumping moralist, although at bottom there is a spiritual element to it. But you do need to have courage and the judgement to know when to make a stand; what battles to fight and what not to. People look for decisiveness in a great leader where other people might haver and duck. A particular issue might be sufficiently important, for an individual or for the culture of a place, that if you do duck it something goes wrong in the community. That could be true in a school or a business organisation, in society or political life.
>
> "Sometimes we see in public life the results of people not having that discernment to see what the moral issues are and the courage to stand on the right side of the line. It's very important that children in a school see – not every day but sometimes in the big moments – somebody being able to articulate that and stand on that right line."

Professional courage

Sudden unexpected events are just one example of how leaders can be blown off course. Such occurrences can undermine confidence and sense of purpose. They demonstrate very clearly why it is not enough to have a vision or a blueprint for your school. You also need the strength to make that vision a reality. Successful headteachers often claim a strong moral force behind their desire to drive through necessary changes. This may be an expression of their faith or ethical values. Invariably it is driven by a deep sense of commitment to children and young people.

Alison Peacock, Headteacher of The Wroxham School in Potters Bar, Hertfordshire, describes it as "professional courage". It is something school leaders need whether faced with exceptional circumstances or simply the constant micro-choices they have to make. In order to be effective, leaders need to know what their core purpose is and have the courage to focus on priorities that really matter.

"I think the notion of professional courage is really key. In order to manage a job which can at times be overwhelming, the way through it is to determine what it is that absolutely requires your attention. The things that require leaders' attention are anything to do with the whole purpose and strategic direction of the school. It's about enabling the vision to come about and leading the learning. It's not about monitoring, it's about understanding the quality of the learning experience the children are having within your school, but also about understanding the learning experience that adults are having as well. For example, how does a new member of staff learn to become part of the team? Do you just leave them to it?

"I spend most of my energy working with people to understand the interactions and the quality of the learning that's going on. That way I'm in a really good position to do some nudging and framing to make sure the core purposes are at the forefront. The courage comes from saying, 'Some of these other things I'm being asked to do can wait because I'm going to do the important things first'. Those things are about the children, the teachers and the community."

Willpower

Madeleine Vigar, Principal of The Castle Partnership Academy Trust, which provides all-through learning at a primary and secondary school in Haverhill, Suffolk, is a classic example of a first-time headteacher who has successfully turned around a previously underperforming school through a mixture of professional courage and willpower.

She recalls how when she went for her interview at Castle Manor Upper School in 2003 she knew that the school "needed a kick up the backside".

"What I found was a staff that were dispirited, demoralised and disempowered. The children really wanted to do well but had completely lost their way and nobody knew how to lead them or to show them the high expectations that were needed. That embodied itself in children in the playground smoking and wearing hoodies; children with Mohican haircuts; children not wearing any uniform whatsoever; staff sitting in two different staffrooms in two different parts of the school looking a bit dispirited, sometimes moaning about the children, sometimes moaning about the 'senior leadership team'. Yet actually the school desperately wanted to do well. There were a lot of people and children who wanted the school to be a success."

She decided that, in order to realise her vision to make the school one of the best in Suffolk, she had to make some rapid changes. She began by listening to the pupils.

"The big changes were firstly about getting children to sit down and behave themselves and to look smart. We agreed as a staff what we would do right at the beginning so, on the very first professional development day I did with staff I arranged for two Year 11 children to come in and tell us what they wanted from their school. That was the first time we ever played, 'What have you done today to make you feel proud?' Those two Year 11s told us what they wanted and we then as a staff decided what we were going to do to improve behaviour. We narrowed it down to a list of six things – simple things such as when children come into a lesson they stand up behind their chairs and wait to be asked to sit down. We put those simple rules on every single wall in the school. The key thing was sticking to them. We didn't do anything else for the first half-term."

Taking a chance

It really helped, she says, that her approach to improving behaviour got publicity in the local media. How she responded showed her appetite for taking a risk on behalf of her pupils and provides a good example of the courage a leader needs to display on occasions to be successful.

"I took a zero-tolerance approach on uniform. There was already a uniform here – it was black sweatshirts and trousers – but no-one ever wore them. They also wore lots of gold jewellery and all sorts of stuff. I made it very clear right from the start, before I took up post, by getting specific staff with new leadership roles to write letters to parents saying that if children arrived on day one and weren't wearing the proper uniform they would be taken out of lessons.

"One boy turned up wearing a sweatshirt with a logo and was taken out of lessons and his father got cross and went to the press. That was quite good for the school because it highlighted what I was trying to do here. A lot of this was about getting the children onside and realising that I was trying to do something quite special for them and that it wasn't just me, it was the rest of the staff as well.

"I decided to take a chance and the next week that boy became the chair of the student council and he appeared in the paper smartly wearing the uniform.

The children liked him. It was one of those quick wins you need to have as a leader. It was something you do by intuition. I'd spent 20 years working in classrooms and as an RE teacher was used to teaching every child in some very big schools. It becomes intuitive that you think, yes, that's how you get them onside. You have to know intuitively about people."

In order to be a good leader you have to be brave and determined, especially coming into a school as a new head, Vigar says. Not only do you have to be prepared to take some very tough decisions but you also have to present yourself as a confident professional, ready to go into battle if necessary.

"You put your suit on every day. When you put your suit on then you're all right because it's your armour. When you've got your suit on and you are in 'headteacher' mode, it's fine, because actually that's what people want to see. You set up an expectation and that's who you are. In a sense that was the whole reason for having a dress code in the school. The children wear their uniforms and that makes them think, 'We're professional, we're business people when we come to school'. It's the same with the staff."

Physical bravery

Sometimes as a school leader you need to show real bravery in order to take charge of a situation that may be personally dangerous, potentially disastrous to the school's reputation, or both. Vigar recalls one incident early in her headship when a real suit of armour would have come in handy.

"My immediate task in the first six months was to keep the school from going into special measures because it was on the verge of doing so. We had a situation in the middle of an Ofsted inspection involving a boy in Year 11 who one of my assistant principals had said was a ticking time bomb. He freaked out and came back into school armed with a golf club to attack another student. It happened right in front of an Ofsted inspector and it could have been a murder. Fortunately it was rescued in time. I got hold of the police quickly as I had already introduced radios as part of those proactive measures that all schools do."

Vigar was able to defuse the situation and two brave teachers put themselves between the threatened pupil and the boy brandishing the golf club until the police moved in.

She says "You look back at the end of the day and you think, 'Gosh did I really do that?' I would never have asked my staff to do those things. After the first six months I did bring in two other members of the leadership team who had worked with me previously who were very well able to deal with those sorts of incidents."

Determination

While physical bravery may be required on occasions leaders need another kind of courage when trying to turn round a troubled school, says Vigar.

"There's a mental courage that you don't waver from. In my case it was the determination that Castle Manor was going to be the best school in Suffolk and that the children there deserved the best. That was the mantra for the school and I passionately believed it. And what I saw when I got here made me believe it more passionately, because I saw children who were completely disempowered and staff that were completely disempowered. There was no reason for it to be anything other than excellent. People make excuses for the failure of schools, but often it's about the conditions that we create in lessons and it's about optimism."

Willingness to take risks

Andrew Hutchinson, Executive Principal of Parkside Federation Academies in Cambridge believes a key aspect of leadership is a willingness to take risks. Having become Headteacher of Parkside Community College, an 11–16 comprehensive in 1999, he became one of the first leaders in the country to form a school federation when he took charge of neighbouring Coleridge Community College in 2005.

"I think as a head you need to be able to stand up and say, 'We have to go somewhere different'. You need to be prepared to be up front and make it clear to people that 'this may not be the easiest way to get there, but it's what we're going to do'. When I did my first set of assemblies for students at Parkside and talked to the staff in 1999 I used the quote from John Kennedy: 'We choose to go to the Moon not because it's easy but because it's hard'. Things that are really worth doing are hard. They involve hard work and risk and that's why we do them and that's the sort of school I wanted us to be; one that would not take the easy options, but would take the hard option – because that's really the way in which you become great.

"There are certain schools where you have to take risks because there is no other alternative, and there are schools that are very safe and can coast along quite nicely. They can be good schools but never move to outstanding because they're not taking the risks."

Willingness to take risks shows a leader has high expectations for a school and is not prepared to settle for relative success, says Hutchinson.

"It's about recognising that you don't really break the mould unless you are prepared to think that the things that are comfortable now aren't going to work in five years' time. It's about being able to take that longer term view. One of the dangers in a school that is relatively successful is that it's easy to think you can just go on incrementally improving what you do, rather than actually saying, 'We'll take some big leaps'. It's not just about the small scale improvements.

"The biggest leap we took was federation with Coleridge in 2005. At the time Parkside was graded outstanding and we had achieved what we had set out to achieve back in 1999. Coleridge was in special measures and about to be closed. It was a massive gamble to decide to do something which at the time was quite rare. We were one of the first schools to take on a failing school and federate with it. We could see the gains of taking that risk were substantial, if we got it right. It was a chance to really change the life chances for school students, double the number of places we were offering and really transform the educational landscape in Cambridge.

"There were a whole host of things that spun off from that. Looking back it was an even bigger risk than we appreciated at the time. There were so many things that could have gone wrong. The school was far worse than we thought it was. It was a case of making that long journey and being prepared to understand that the medium and long-term gains would be hugely significant in terms of Parkside and Coleridge. The fact that we now have a federation, we're ready to open a third school [a new secondary school due to open in Trumpington in 2015] and have opened a successful sixth form as well shows the benefits for the community. We were prepared to take the ultimate risk to turn around something which had a systemic history of failure."

Broadening horizons

Risk aversion is a common symptom of schools that are in trouble. When Devon Hanson took on the headship of Walworth Academy in Southwark in 2007 he was appalled at the lack of opportunities open to pupils to stimulate learning, broaden horizons and raise aspirations. What he discovered was an inward-looking school with a 'can't do' culture.

"You have to be courageous and determined and you have to be able to take risks. You have to take risks with people and you have to take risks with the children. When I came to Walworth some children had been at the school for five years and never been on a school trip. During my first term, Year 9 pupils were doing *A Midsummer Night's Dream*. Children learn better if they can see something visual. So I wanted them to go and watch the play but the teachers said, 'No Sir, we don't take them out because they're too poorly behaved'. I said, 'We are taking them out, find a theatre'. So they found a theatre somewhere in the West End but I said 'No, that's too close'. The only other one was in Canterbury and I said, 'That's the one they're going to'. They said, 'Why Canterbury?' I said I wanted to broaden the children's horizons and to get them to start thinking that there's a wider world out there other than SE1 or SE13 where they live.

"I wanted them to go on a journey and to see that there were open spaces in Kent within half an hour of where they live. You could hear a pin drop on the coach on that trip because they were so intrigued. They kept going, 'Wow, wow!' Everywhere we went after that the managers of theatres and other places would invariably say how brilliantly our children had behaved. But it was a big risk."

This is exactly the kind of professional courage that Alison Peacock describes. At the core of Hanson's vision is the determination to "live equal opportunities". He wanted children at Walworth to be able to have the same sort of experiences and opportunities routinely offered to children who go to independent schools. And he did not want those opportunities to be denied because of fears about discipline.

> "I also sent our modern languages children across to France when previously the attitude was 'Why bother, when our children don't want to learn languages anyway?' I said we had got to motivate them to want to learn. So we arranged a study visit to a school and a museum so that they would see that young people in France dress like them and do everything the same as them. The only difference is that they talk a different language. It helps them to understand that it's not a bad thing at all to learn a language, that with careers and globalisation you don't have to be working in the same area that you come from. It may well be that you have to move abroad. It makes them realise the value of broadening their horizons."

Dealing with underperforming staff

Among the hardest aspects of leadership is dealing with staff members who are underperforming. Sue Hargadon, Principal of Farlingaye High School in Woodbridge, Suffolk, says this is one of the most critical aspects of leadership. It is, she says, something that distinguishes the role of headteacher or principal from that of deputy head – the knowledge that the buck stops with you.

"One of the things I will do which I don't think all school leaders do is challenge incompetence and I think that's the big difference between headship and being a deputy head. Often a deputy still needs to be liked by people but when you become a head you recognise that you have to challenge people and take them on. I think that's the hardest part of what you do and I don't know if all heads do it."

This view is shared by Ani Magill, Headteacher of St John the Baptist School in Woking, Surrey, who says:

> "One of the things heads often really lack is they talk about making the tough decisions, but actually when it comes down to looking somebody in the eye and saying 'I'm sorry it's not good enough, you've got to go', that's the bit they avoid. I don't think you can ever be a great leader unless you've got the courage to have those conversations. That courage also has to be based on the belief that we are here to serve the children and to make sure the children get a good deal because if you don't deep down believe that then where are you going to find the courage to make those tough decisions?"

Llyn Codling, Executive Headteacher at Portswood and St Mary's Church of England primary schools in Southampton, agrees. "Some of the most difficult decisions you have to make are when people are not teaching as well as they should be and you need to have a courageous conversation about the next steps,' she says.

> "You have done all you can to support them to improve, but then you have got to sit down with them. It doesn't mean you have to be horrible, you just have to think about how you are going to do it and not avoid it. We all know headteachers who have avoided that and therefore have got teachers where you think, 'Why is that teacher still teaching?' when they should have been provided with support to improve or if that doesn't work to move out. I always talk about Jim Collins's [business coach and author of *Good to Great* (Random House, 2001)] analogy about getting the right people on the bus. Sometimes you have to stop the bus and let people off. And that's the courageous bit: stopping the bus and letting people off."

Tackling children's behaviour

Headteachers also need to be willing to step in and support their staff when problems arise concerning children's behaviour.

"It's about having conversations with parents who are absolutely convinced their child is being bullied and really don't want to see that their child is being equally unkind to someone else," says Codling.

"You have to unpick the word bullying which is really emotive and try to remove the emotion and try and get a balanced judgement and that can be very hard because we are dealing with people's children. We are dealing with their most precious thing in their lives so emotions come into play. Trying to get that balance between having the courage to say what needs to be said and being sensitive to those emotions can be really hard."

Willingness to take on difficult behavioural issues and provide support is something staff members expect and really appreciate from a headteacher, says Sue Hargadon.

> "I don't know if its courage you need, but it's about tackling behaviour. That's what the staff most want – to know that they've got your full support in tackling behaviour. I think sometimes the most courageous thing you do is tackling

difficult parents – when you have a really difficult child and you know that whatever action you take you are going to have a horrendous phone call from a parent and there's this huge temptation to back off. That's where the courage comes in."

Farlingaye High School is now Suffolk's biggest secondary school with over 1,900 pupils and under Hargadon's leadership it attained an 'outstanding' grading from Ofsted in 2007. But when she took over as headteacher in 1996 it was relatively small, with just over 1,100 pupils. In those early days she found the behaviour of some pupils "surprisingly challenging" and had to deal with several major incidents. One in particular required all her fortitude.

"I had a child push another child through a bus window and I called the police in and that resulted in the parents getting involved. It was one of those horrible nightmare situations where you think, 'God what have I taken on here?' I suppose that was about courage, because it meant telling everybody that I was not going to back off, that I will be there to be counted and I was really glad I did it. I can remember going home and not sleeping all that weekend I was so worried about what I'd done and whether I'd taken the right action."

Seeking advice

Incidents such as these are part and parcel of being a school leader and how you deal with them will tell other people in your school community a great deal about what kind of place you want your school to be. On such occasions it is important to be firm and, whenever possible, seek out advice from other experienced leaders.

"I would say it was like that for five or six years. I was going home and discussing everything with my poor husband – and now the same sort of things might happen but I've just got used to it. I know that things will sort themselves out," says Hargadon.

"It doesn't mean I don't still worry about it but I have a perspective on it now which comes with experience and which you don't have as a new head. I often find it's quite flattering that newer heads, particularly ones that have come through my school, will ring me up for advice about a particular incident. I still get hugely upset about things but I've got a lot more resilience now."

Staying firm under pressure

Being prepared to hold firmly to one's principles under pressure is one of the most critical characteristics of successful headship says Maggie Farrar, former Executive Director of the National College for School Leadership.

"Leaders are the ones who will hold on to doing what is right even if others wobble. Great leaders have a deep sense of moral purpose and have a set of inner core principles which they measure everything against. They know what is the right thing to do and are steadfast. There is a steadfastness in leaders that people in schools really value," she says.

According to Andrew Fleck, Headmaster of Sedbergh School, an independent boarding school in Cumbria, headship is often about achieving objectives against the odds. Leaders constantly have to battle against conflicting demands and people who tell them that things they are trying to achieve cannot be done, he says.

> "Nobody tells you what it feels like to carry the burden 24 hours a day. No preparation that I can think of totally equips you for that. The resilience required – and it is emotional as well as physical – is considerable. I certainly found in my first year of headship that I became exhausted and my resilience dipped considerably. Determination comes in so many forms. It's very easy to come in as a new head and say, 'This is my view of how things should change or develop'. The energy and commitment required to see even what may seem a simple thing through to an outcome is enormous because it's about overcoming perception problems, competing priorities and resource issues. It's about communicating clearly and winning the argument, particularly with academic staff, as well as pupils, parents, governors and bursars.
>
> "To see something through to its conclusion and implementation is pretty demanding. You have to be committed and resolute that it is the right thing to do. Fatigue can sap that. Particularly as a new school leader, it's so important to choose one's first projects – or battles, if they turn out that way – wisely, because not only will people be gauging the wisdom of the decision but also the determination of the new incumbent to see something through. If you can see something through successfully and cleanly then the team will follow you in the future. That's terribly important."

A willingness to challenge

An important quality in a school leader is a willingness to challenge received opinion. This applies as much to a school that is already successful but ripe for further development as one that is struggling at the foot of the performance tables.

In 2008 Bernard Trafford, who had already been Headmaster of Wolverhampton Grammar School for 18 years – was appointed Headmaster of the Royal Grammar School in Newcastle. Even with two decades of senior leadership under his belt he found the going tough at first.

"When you come in as a new head everything – and I mean almost everything except the nice bits – conspires to push you off course unless you have the courage to make the necessary changes. You have to have courage to do the awful bits of being a head, particularly the disciplinaries, whether with children or with teachers. The place where we famously lack courage as leaders is in dealing with under-performing teachers. If you are trying to move a school on people don't like change. You come in with this vision for the school and that's why they appoint you.

"I came to the Royal Grammar School which was already a high-achieving school and I reckoned it should be achieving a bit more highly academically. It was just a feeling that we should be sharper, more imaginative, less playing safe. It doesn't half annoy people when you say that. You have to be brave and say 'No, we are going to work on this, we are going to push this way'. It would be a lot easier not to.

"Of course it wasn't only me. There were people in my senior team who wanted to change things and hadn't been able to. I've got a Director of Studies who was very keen that we should really concentrate on learning instead of worrying about teaching. The state sector had been doing that for at least a decade. Teachers don't like to be told they need to change and they'll fight back and so it wasn't easy. We focused on learning and then we moved on to review the curriculum. Any curriculum shake-up is quite stressful as it inevitably involves vested interests. Nobody will let go of the status quo if they can help it unless it's better for them. So moving from teaching to learning was a fundamental change. It was threatening even though it shouldn't be. People are human and you have to be sensitive about their feelings. I found it quite tough, even as an experienced head. Change is always hard work and always annoys people."

Energy, courage and perseverance

Paul Smith, Principal of Parbold Douglas Church of England Academy, a primary school in Lancashire, is another admirer of the business coach and author Jim Collins and quotes approvingly from his bestselling book, *Good to Great* (Random House, 2001): "Few people attain great lives, in large part because it is just so easy to settle for a good life". In order to achieve necessary changes a school leader has to have energy, courage and perseverance, says Smith.

"You need courage and perseverance whether you are taking on a school in a very challenging situation, or a good or outstanding school, because there will be challenges that you have to overcome. To take on those challenges, energy is very important because it will take a lot of your time. Often significant change can seem like the worst possible idea, especially just before it starts to become embedded and bring about the improvement that you intended it to have. Perseverance comes from knowing that you have made the right decision, and can stay the course. I think that's absolutely essential because when you do make a decision to make significant or major changes you will have people coming at you from all sides. People will question you or confront you and tell you that what you are doing is wrong.

"Change is a difficult thing to manage, but that's our job as school leaders and if we turn up every day and just maintain things as they are then we're not really leading the school. We are maintaining it, or managing it and I think a true leader sees the potential to move it forward."

Taking time

While courage and determination are important characteristics in a school leader, however, it is important to remember that major change takes time to achieve. Determination to drive innovation needs to be tempered by patience. You need to take "the long view while also dealing with blocking and frustration" as you go along, says Bernard Trafford.

"It's astonishing how long it can take to change anything. The good thing is that two or three years on you look back and think, 'Blimey, we have moved a long way'. But it takes time. You need patience, but also impatience as well, to push things forward."

You also need to be able to remain calm under pressure. Just as Richard Harman took the time for quiet reflection before taking action over bullying at Uppingham, Trafford's no-nonsense advice is always to pause before you leap to a decision you might otherwise come to regret.

"Whenever there is a crisis people want it sorting out immediately. I once came across this command: 'Don't just do something, sit there!' It's great advice because actually it's usually better to sleep on it and not rush in whenever you are faced with anything difficult. People so often want it sorted straight away and they don't like it when you say 'We're not rushing in'. But usually you get a much better result."

3
Passion

Successful school leaders are passionate about teaching and learning and show great commitment to children and young people.

Madeleine Vigar had been a teacher for 20 years when, in 2002, she decided to take a break from the profession. As an experienced deputy head she was already on course for headship. Yet when the opportunity arose for her to work in industry she jumped at the chance.

After two decades in the profession it was a chance to try something different with the option of returning to school leadership after a year or making a permanent career change. She went to work for a construction company and spent 12 months working with architects, surveyors and financial experts on a number of school building projects funded by the government's private finance initiative (PFI).

"I learned some interesting lessons about industry but decided after a year that it wasn't for me. I realised that actually education was in my blood and I wanted to come back into schools. There was always a plan that I would come back into headship if I didn't like leadership in industry," she says.

She found herself missing the constant interactions of school life and realised working with children and teachers was her real passion. So she returned, feeling refreshed and ready to spend the rest of her career in the profession. In September 2003, she took up an appointment as Headteacher of Castle Manor Community Upper School in Haverhill, Suffolk, which was underperforming and in danger of being placed in special measures. While it took courage and determination to take the school on its subsequent journey – under her leadership and the new name of Castle Manor Business and Enterprise College it was graded 'outstanding' by Ofsted in 2010 – it also required considerable dedication. That, she says now, can only come if you have real passion for the job.

A true vocation

"I love what I do. I can't imagine not doing it. That's why I stopped it after 20 years, to see if I could do something different and I was lost. The year I had out in industry was boring by comparison. I missed having people to bounce ideas off; all those interactions you get every day in a school. You suddenly think, 'I'm turning into Miss Jean Brody'. You suddenly find yourself at 50 thinking, 'How did this happen?' because it gets in your blood. You have to have that passion. There's nothing better than seeing a child that you thought was going in the wrong direction, having switched round and doing something really amazing. That has not left me from the moment I became an RE teacher. As a school leader, it's your job to radiate that to others."

Having a passionate interest in the job of teaching and, by extension, of leading a school, raises the question of whether the profession is a vocation or not. One of the most common replies from successful leaders, when asked what key quality is needed to run a good school, is 'Liking children and showing it'. If there is a true vocation to teach and progress to headship then that is surely it. The passion many of these leaders show for their craft and their desire to help children achieve their best is perhaps the quality that defines them most clearly. It is the quality that brought them into teaching in the first place and which sustains them and informs their actions throughout the daily grind of headship.

Vigar joined the profession as a religious education teacher in the early 1980s, having under-achieved at school. She believes her love of teaching, which blossomed when she found herself in charge of a class of children for the first time, stems from not having had the best educational experiences herself.

"I was surprised that I was going to be an RE teacher because I was so badly behaved at school. But I discovered that I was really quite passionate about getting children to think and to learn to debate and discuss, and RE was ideal for that. From thereon in I realised that being a teacher meant you had some influence and ability to change people's lives. Becoming a headteacher was never something I had planned. It just happened really. What drives it is the major belief that I want to do a job that makes a difference. That probably sounds a bit twee, but it's something that's just in you, that you feel you want to do."

She believes her own background, which included a long period of unhappiness after her father died when she was nine, has given her a natural empathy which helps her to motivate children who are disaffected or struggling to achieve.

"I speak to children who misbehave sometimes and occasionally have been very naughty and I say to them, 'Look, I didn't have the best start in life either. Believe me you're not the only one who's had a hard time, but what are you going to do about it?' Where does that sort of passion come from? Why is it that leaders will get up early in the morning and work long hours? What is that all about?"

Another leader whose passion for education stems from her upbringing is Lynn Slinger, Headteacher of Forest Way Special School in Coalville, Leicestershire. Having grown up on a Sheffield council estate, she went to the local grammar school thanks partly to a German mother who had high aspirations for her daughter. The school became a comprehensive the following year so she gained an insight into both selective and non-selective education. Her working class background gave her an interest, initially, in becoming a social worker but she finally decided instead to train as a teacher.

"I did my teacher training in Leicester and it was just so fascinating I stayed with it. I trained to be a primary teacher and my first class was almost completely Ugandan Asians who had moved to Leicester. That was an absolutely fantastic learning experience for me. I started working in a primary school in Leicester and became very interested in ethnic minorities, the way they struggled to learn at first because of their English and how well they did subsequently because of their backgrounds and their parents' high aspirations for them.

"I also became very interested in special needs so from there I went to teach in a special school teaching children with severe learning disabilities. The first week I just came home in tears every day and I thought it wasn't for me because I just found it so upsetting seeing so many children with disabilities in one place. I just couldn't cope with it. But by the end of the week I began to see the personalities beyond the disabilities and realised that was what it was all about and that it was something that really excited me trying to help these children to achieve."

Special challenge

After working as a teacher and senior leader in a number of challenging schools, she was offered the headship of Forest Way in 1994. At the time it was a small special school and her initial impression was that it was very successful and well managed. That changed, however, when she took up the post and realised the job was much bigger than she had anticipated.

"I had seen some very challenging schools but the whole culture of the school was unlike anything I had ever experienced before. Staff brought sick children into school on sick beds. Staff brought dogs into school. Staff swapped children between classes as they wanted to. They didn't stick to a timetable. There were no set procedures that people stuck to. There was no clear leadership. There was no confidentiality. I had got two job share deputies who didn't get on with each other, so I didn't have a strong leadership team.

"My big strength was the governing body. They were committed to me and they were committed to making the school the best it could possibly be. So they were fully supportive. If it hadn't been for them I wouldn't have been able to do the job that needed doing to improve the quality of teaching which really was very archaic and old fashioned. There was a big culture of caring for the children but education was something that needed to be developed. I wanted both the education and the care. I didn't want it to be like a hospital, I wanted it to be a very caring school."

Her vision was to make it the best special school in the country and a real centre of excellence, an ambitious project for a school in a former mining community like Coalville. She set in motion a series of changes designed to create the kind of climate she wanted for the school.

"I wanted it to feel purposeful and happy. The old Forest Way was happy but it wasn't purposeful. I wanted every child to achieve the best they could achieve in a very happy environment but I wanted them to be stretched. I didn't want any cosiness. Just because a child has got a disability it doesn't mean they should not be pushed to do the best they can do. I wanted a real sense of excitement, a buzz. I wanted the children still to be cared for medically or physically but I also wanted to push them to their limits whatever that might be individually to enable them to achieve the best they could.

"I also wanted the staff to achieve their best. I wanted really exciting staff who were stimulated and who really wanted to come to work every day and still be excited by the job."

Many headteachers and principals speak of the importance of having drive and energy to do their job effectively and of being ambitious on behalf of their school. Such determination to make a school the best it can be is often driven by a leader's passion to create the right conditions for children to flourish. Creating that sense of enthusiasm and excitement can be a powerful motivational force for both staff and pupils.

Slinger puts it this way: "A lot of people have said to me, 'Oh your passion comes through and when we talk to you it really buoys us up'. I would say I am passionate and people have said the passion is very obvious. People have also said to me, 'Oh you have been in the job for 18 years; that must be really boring', but actually it's never boring. The job changes every day and if it was boring why would I still be here?"

Her passion for her job has taken Forest Way Special School a long way. Twice graded as 'outstanding' by Ofsted, it is now housed in a purpose-built, eco-friendly building and is hugely popular with parents. As a National Teaching School it influences teaching and learning in 25 other schools and as a National Support School it also works with under-performing schools.

Her success as a leader and considerable responsibilities beyond her own school mean her interests and opportunities to influence others have grown so that she is now much more focused on the bigger picture. Even so, her passion remains firmly centred on helping children.

"My first passion is for the children. At the heart of everything I do is the children and that's the passion that drove me initially. But now, actually, having seen the effect having a school with such a fantastic reputation has on the children, staff, the community as a whole and other local schools, I realise I'm actually passionate for learning in the community. It started with just being the children at this school but it's expanded into a much broader passion. Now I am also involved nationally and I realise how much that can bring back into the school and the impact it can have on the children. I can also influence national policy which affects children in a much wider sense. So I think my passion started in a very-focused way in the school, but actually now it's about education as a whole."

For the majority of leaders, this passion for helping children fulfil their potential is the essential ingredient in any successful school. It is something that should be present at every level, from the newly-qualified teacher or classroom assistant through to the headteacher or principal.

Commitment to young people

Patricia Scott, Headteacher of St Luke's High School in Barrhead, East Renfrewshire – one of the highest performing comprehensives in Scotland despite its above-average share of children eligible for free meals – believes a passionate commitment to young people is 'the core business' of any school.

"That's what should be at the centre of everything. I'm very well aware that there is this huge responsibility for me, as headteacher, but it's the same for everyone who has an interaction with young people in the school. Children only get one chance at formal education, so everyone who has that interaction has that opportunity and privilege to affect the learning and the lifelong learning of youngsters in school. The role they play and the passion they bring to the job is absolutely critical for a school's success," she says.

It is the headteacher's responsibility to show that passion and commitment by being visible throughout the school day, taking an interest in pupils' work, recognising achievements and interacting with staff.

"It's absolutely critical that you know the children well, that they know you, and they know that you care about them, in good and bad times. It's not just teaching subjects that we're dealing with; it's about young people's lives in all their complexity and all of the challenges that happen inside the school building. It's the wider life and community that youngsters are coping with too – as they mature through their education."

As an example she describes a typical day at her school.

"I would spend much of the day with youngsters from very early in the morning – meeting them coming into school. I'll be in front of the school every morning as youngsters are coming off school buses, walking into school, socialising and getting themselves organised – all the mundane things, but all those things that are absolutely critical to a good start to the day for youngsters. At other points throughout the day I can be in the classes. I do a lot of learning walks across the school, watching youngsters at work. In classes, I would be looking at things like collecting in their student planners and looking at how well organised they are.

"There are lots of things you can pick up from the school planners, the amount of homework that they have, the level of organisation for things they are getting involved in. Our own planners have things like achievement sheets and I would be looking at whether they are recognising children's achievements and recording them. That would allow me to have that conversation with them and to celebrate their achievements with them.

"Every morning we have assembly for each year group which we spend leading them in the school prayer, but also celebrating their successes with them, the things they've been doing in terms of learning and teaching projects or anything else that we wanted to share at that particular time. I also see them in social areas at break times, in the canteen at lunchtime and so on and again at the end of the day, making sure that everyone is safely onto buses and away. So we spend a lot of time in and around youngsters every day."

Being open and approachable

A crucial aspect of this approach is to show that you are open and approachable as a leader and that you are knowledgeable and enthusiastic about what is going on in your school. It is also an opportunity to model that enthusiasm and to get pupils and staff passionate about their teaching and learning.

"It's important to be visible around the school at all times. I think that's really important for the pupils and for the staff. It's also important to show that you support them, that you are interested and concerned about what they're doing and that you know what's going on. What that results in is that staff and pupils will feel they're comfortable to say 'Oh we're doing X, Y and Z on such and such a day, will you come along and see it?' It shows that you're involved in their learning. You might not be there teaching them in the classroom on the day but you are there involved in the learning and you can see how they are progressing. I think that's very important.

"It's also important for staff to be able to showcase their practice as well and by having that kind of presence around the school it also encourages other staff to do the same thing. That means they are not simply going from the staffroom to the classroom. They are interested in what's going on round and about the social areas with the youngsters, they're looking at one another's practice in the classroom and that becomes an accepted and a natural way of going about learning and teaching in the school, in a very open and mature way."

Motivating pupils and staff

Devon Hanson, who in 2012 left Walworth Academy to take up a new headship at another ARK Schools academy, Evelyn Grace Academy in Brixton, says that leaders need to be able to express their passion for teaching and learning at all times. Showing that you are enthusiastic about what is happening in your school is a powerful way of inspiring and motivating pupils and staff.

"That has to be at the heart of it because even if you are tired, no matter how you feel, you have to show an enthusiastic face, you have got to be up for it, you cannot be walking with your head down not looking at children, not saying hello to teachers. Even if you just say hello. The amount of headteachers I see that walk past their teachers without saying anything, that's not good. Once you start acknowledging people as part of your passion to show them how you feel, you are doing your job.

"Headteachers have got to show passion. When you are doing assemblies you've got to think not only what you are saying to children but somehow a line has got to be in there for teachers. Your motivational qualities have got to be primed and you've got to utilise every instance. So I utilise assemblies where I might do something on 'hope' and I will say it for the children but I know that will transcend to some teachers and they often come back to me and say they've learned from it. I did an assembly on climbing a mountain and teachers came back to me and said, 'Yes, today my mountain will be 9C3. I didn't teach them too well last lesson and they're my mountain today and I'm going to climb it'.

"You always have to include teachers in everything you do because you try to motivate pupils but it is equally important to motivate the teachers as well."

When Hanson was appointed to his first headship at Walworth School, Southwark, in 2007, the school was struggling. Under his leadership, the school converted to an academy and achieved a dramatic rise in the proportion of pupils gaining five or more GCSE A*–C grades, including English and mathematics (up from 26 per cent in 2007 to 70 per cent in 2011). In 2010, Ofsted rated it as a good school with outstanding capacity for sustained improvement.

One of the most important qualities needed to turn round a school in difficulties, he says, is for a leader to show their passion and commitment to everyone in the school, especially to the children.

"I think you have to stand straight and you have to be able to deliver. You can be an office-space headteacher which I would never support. I walk into the classes, I walk round the corridors. I stand at the door, at the gates in the mornings and evenings. What's also important is to know the children as individuals. If I see a group of five children as long as I know one of their names the other four will think I know them as well. I always find a way to acknowledge. If you are in the playground that's their domain so talk with them, smile with them. Say to them, 'Hello young man', 'hello young lady' as you walk by. Those children will do as much for you in the classroom because they know you respect them when they see you outside the classroom."

The ability to enthuse and motivate teachers and support staff is equally important and can be far more effective than taking a confrontational approach, Hanson believes.

"My aim is to get passion, to get the professional integrity and get the teachers to really stretch themselves and to ask the pupils to stretch themselves. Many of the new academies that were being set up when I came to Walworth appointed a new team. I brought in one other person apart from myself. I worked with the same teachers and if they were disaffected I worked with them to get them motivated. In the first year, the same teachers and the pupils increased their GCSE results by 10 percentage points. After the first year we lost a few teachers, some who didn't want to work for an academy and some who just didn't make the grade, but they left with good feelings and good intentions. They didn't leave with animosity or hatred for me. They knew where we were going and they knew it was going to require a sense of commitment and skill and knowledge and that I was going to be relentless with a smile and with passion.

"They knew there was no other agenda, there was nothing personal with anybody, but the children's lives were important. What was amazing was that the staff changed but you would never know it. There weren't any big union battles, there weren't any teachers taking out grievances. Teachers knew that this school, with me, was going places, and if they weren't up to it then they should do the honourable thing."

One of the key motivational factors in this approach was the invitation to 'buy in' to the project to raise standards. While there was clearly an element of tough love accompanying the passion the intention was to get the staff to make the same commitment Hanson himself was ready to make. The reward would be a career investment in a rapidly improving school.

"I told the teachers when I first came here that if I hadn't made the difference within two years I would leave. I also told them, 'It's pointless for you at this stage applying for jobs, even if you are good, because you are coming from a failing school and no headteacher would look at you. But if you stick with me for two years – this was in 2007 – in 2009 everybody would want you'."

Passion for children's learning

Maggie Farrar, former Executive Director of the National College for School Leadership, believes leaders need to be able to demonstrate their passion for children's learning in every aspect of their work.

"They display and demonstrate a real love of children and an enthusiasm for the learning that goes on in schools. Underneath all that is what the day-to-day actions are to show that this is true. I meet good heads all the time who can go into every classroom, tell me something about every teacher, know every child by name, know what is going on, is delighted and enthusiastic about what children are doing. That's what you need to see on a daily basis," she says.

Even in the largest secondary schools, such as Farlingaye High School in Woodbridge, Suffolk, with over 1,900 pupils, it is important for the leader to be able to connect with individual children and staff. Children especially need to feel valued and cared for, says the Principal Sue Hargadon.

"Caring passionately about children as individuals is really important. It's important that I know that the parents of my school think I know their children and I care about them and even if I don't know them directly, I will deal with any problem they have because I care. Staff also want to know that you care personally about them."

One of the reasons many teachers turn their backs on the chance to move into senior leadership is their love of teaching. Successful leaders, however, seize upon the opportunities of headship to influence young lives on a much larger scale. That is one of the best aspects of the job, says Hargadon.

> "What I love about teaching is that no two days are ever the same. I just think kids are fabulous and they need you and make you smile. The nice thing about being a head is the feeling that you can change things. People often say, don't you miss the classroom? And you do, but actually you can start making a difference to a much wider range of children. In my own classroom I can make a difference to the children I teach but once you become a head you can start making teaching and learning worthwhile for everyone in the school."

Bernard Trafford, Headmaster of the Royal Grammar School in Newcastle, takes a similar view. He believes that leaders need to be able to convey a sense of excitement, in much the same way as a teacher does, in order to inspire children to perform at their best.

> "I was a music teacher. I was pretty mad in the 1980s and over the top. There was a huge excitement in what we were doing. Why did I want to be a head? It was because I could do it on a bigger scale than just the music department. There is the same buzz when it's good, when you feel it's going the right way and especially when children are surprising themselves in what they can achieve in every sphere of activity. When that happens there is the same excitement and passion as you get as a classroom teacher, but on a bigger scale."

Passion and moral purpose

Teresa Tunnadine, Headteacher of The Compton School in North London, is another example of a leader whose career was founded on a deep passion for teaching children, even though she initially battled against going into the profession.

"After university I went into the civil service, but decided that was not fulfilling enough for me. My mother was a teacher and everyone has always said to me, 'You want to go into teaching'. I fought it for about three years and then decided to go for it. I loved it from the word go. Quite quickly I moved into middle leadership, after about three years, and into senior leadership after about six years. I taught geography. I became a head of year and then a senior teacher in a huge 1,600-pupil merged school in North London, where I have always worked – in urban, multi-ethnic mixed comprehensives. After six years as a senior teacher doing a range of jobs I applied for a deputy headship at the school I am at now."

For her, being passionate about children's lives is a fundamental requirement in a school leader.

"It's what you feel when you see some children who come in and the fact that they even arrive in school is extraordinary. They might come from a place where there's no food in the fridge or there's no one to look after them or they are a carer for a parent who is ill. Some of these children have extraordinary lives and you cannot help but be passionate about wanting to give them the very best because they deserve it and they need it. It goes back to moral purpose. Each member of staff who comes to my school to teach has that passion. If you are a teacher in a very good school your opportunities for fulfilment in the job and your chances of advancement and promotion are much higher. I am passionate about the staff we have as well as the children. But fundamentally it's about the children. You cannot help but be compelled by the importance of this job when you see the children coming in every day. So it is about passion and it is about moral purpose. The two I think are the same."

Like many of the best school leaders, Tunnadine is proud to be a teacher and believes that classroom experience is an essential preparation for running a school. As a headteacher she continues to draw upon her own teaching practice and understanding of children and always tries to stay in touch with their needs and feelings.

> "For me it works, and has done from the moment I set foot in the classroom and was developing relationships and getting to know children as individuals and really enjoying working with children and seeing them develop socially and intellectually. It means that when I'm doing the job that I now do I can constantly refer back to the job that I did as a classroom teacher. It's back to moral purpose and having experience of what a difference schools can make to children. Even in the dark days it makes it all worthwhile.
>
> "So for me, I have to keep reminding myself why I do this job and why it's so important. I have my own consultation groups. I have groups of children that I meet with on a regular basis to keep me grounded so I know what they are thinking and feeling and what the important issues are for them. It wouldn't have worked for me if I hadn't had that background as a teacher. It means I also know the pressures and the tensions the staff are under and also the positives. It helps that I have done all the jobs in school so that I can relate to what people have to do."

Should school leaders be teachers?

Most successful school leaders unquestionably see their mission as rooted in an understanding of pedagogy and a commitment to:

- teaching
- learning
- subject knowledge.

They believe helping their pupils to achieve their best and to develop into well-rounded individuals is what running a school is all about. Yet recent changes in the way schools are organised and administered, especially in England, raise questions about whether the school leaders of the future should necessarily be teachers at all. As increasing numbers of schools opt for independence from local authorities and form new alliances as part of federations or multi-academy chains, the role of school leader is becoming increasingly complex.

Even the term 'headteacher' has disappeared in many of England's schools as growing numbers of academies emerge under the leadership of principals. In addition, new forms of leadership have developed with the terms 'executive principal', 'executive headteacher' and 'chief executive' becoming increasingly common. Academy chains are typically run by a chief executive officer, advised by a director of education, in much the same way as the local authorities which they are gradually eclipsing. In December 2011, the British government scrapped the requirement for new headteachers and principals to have a professional headship qualification, in the form of the National Professional Qualification for Headship (NPQH), a move that in theory at least opens the way for schools to be led by people with no teaching background.

A hands-on role

As these changes gather pace, however, arguably the real debate is not about whether leaders should be qualified teachers but whether those with executive responsibilities for a number of schools can realistically maintain a hands-on role. Can they keep that connection much treasured by many of the most successful leaders or should they step back and delegate responsibility for teaching and learning?

Nicola Shipman, Executive Headteacher of Fox Hill, Mansel and Monteney Primary Schools in Sheffield, is one successful leader who has faced this dilemma. She has always been passionate about teaching and went into the profession despite the best efforts of her parents (both teachers) to deter her. After being appointed Headteacher of Monteney Primary in 2003, she took the school first to 'good' and then to 'outstanding' in successive Ofsted inspections.

In 2007, she was asked by Sheffield City Council to support a neighbouring primary school, Fox Hill, then in special measures, and in 2009 the two schools formed a federation with Shipman as Executive Head. In 2012, she also began working with Mansel Primary, at the time the lowest-performing school in the city. All three schools serve disadvantaged communities in the same part of Sheffield, with a high proportion of families on low incomes.

The role necessarily means her dividing her time between the schools and has forced her to delegate some of her responsibilities to other leaders.

"The one aspect of my role I really struggle with now being an executive head is not knowing all the children's names. I really prided myself on that and being, I suppose, the headteacher figure that I remember my headteacher being. I think the nature of school leadership has changed significantly and very reluctantly I have resigned myself to the fact that, leading a chain of schools, I can't always be the face of the school that children and parents can turn to. However, whenever I'm in school I'm always visible, always there for the parents and always there for the children.

"Having that desire, that interaction, is really important for everyone who works in a school. When we interview people, we ask them 'Why Monteney?', 'Why do you want this job?' When somebody says 'It's something I've always wanted to do' I really used to think that was corny. Now I actually don't think it's corny, I think it's really important."

For many leaders in this rapidly evolving system, this dilemma of how to stay in touch with children, ensure that they are being well taught by teachers who are passionate about their work, while carrying out their wider executive responsibilities, is a real one. Shipman has resolved the difficulty by creating a leadership team that can take on her role whenever she is out of school.

"It's been a bit of a journey to get over the fact that I can't do every single assembly in three schools on a Monday morning – that is a physical impossibility. But I know that somebody else can, and they do it very well."

CEO or headteacher?

Paul Smith, Principal of Parbold Douglas Church of England Academy, a large village primary school in Lancashire, believes firmly that the modern school leader's role is more that of a chief executive than headteacher.

"I am not a headteacher, I'm a principal. I don't teach and I have a deputy who looks after teaching and learning. I would argue that a headteacher is a Victorian throwback to when you had someone responsible for the quality of teaching and learning and that was their only job. Then when local management of schools came in 20 years ago the role of the headteacher changed. I think the term 'headteacher' is outdated now if you think of it in terms of the lead teacher in a school. I defy any headteacher, even in a small school, to act as a lead teacher. They might act as a class teacher for part of the week, but when they are not in class they have to deal with finance, buildings, grounds, contractors and contracts. Much more of my time is spent on that than on education. I have a vice-principal who does that."

The principal's role, argues Smith, is not to relinquish responsibility for the strategic direction of the school but to create the conditions in which others can take day-to-day control of teaching and learning.

"That's the importance of the team. It's important to be able to recognise that. My deputy, my head of curriculum, is there to do that and she does it far better than me. In many ways my position is almost political – I'm there to make people comfortable and happy and convince them that this is the right thing to do. I insist that the quality of teaching and learning is high and I ask my deputy the right questions at the right time. I still have that quality assurance in there – but I'm not going to go in and teach alongside one of my teachers to improve their performance – that's not my job. That's the deputy's job so she actually is the lead or 'head teacher' of the school. I'm the CEO of the organisation and she's ultimately answerable to me."

Attention to detail

Andrew Hutchinson, Executive Principal of Parkside Federation Academies in Cambridge, is responsible for two 11 to 16 schools and a combined sixth form, each of which has a headteacher. He believes that in order to run a school effectively even the busiest executive head needs to pay rigorous attention to detail. That requires them to be highly visible in their schools.

"So many little things matter and they go together to make the big things. It matters what the reception area looks like, it matters what the playground looks like, it matters how people present themselves. All those little elements go together. That's not in the sense of zero-tolerance policy that some schools work on, where every detail of the uniform is monitored. We've always viewed it more as a commitment to the highest quality, ensuring that we do things for a reason. Once we know what that reason is we expect there to be a commitment to deliver at every level. It's equally important that the site team cares about making sure there is no rubbish lying about and the students do the same. That needs to be hammered home again and again. By keeping those small things in people's eyes the big things often follow more easily.

"As a head it is important to be able to be on the shop floor to see what happens there and then as well as to understand how it's working at the top level. If you get the top and the bottom right then the middle often looks after itself. If you work at a set of structures at the top and you work at the ground floor to make sure the delivery is as you think it should be the middle is where you can allow innovation and give people the opportunity to develop their own skills."

While these organisational skills are vital in a school leader, however, it is the underlying purpose that really matters.

"I think that a lot of good heads have an obsession with doing it absolutely right at all levels. It could be viewed as micro-management. There is a danger that as a head you can become a micro-manager and I think the heads that get it right are those that don't necessarily micro-manage, they micro-care. They care about the detail – and encourage others to care about the detail, rather than trying to do all the detail. If you try to do it all yourself you will fall apart. It's imparting that sense that the details matter."

This passion about creating the right conditions for teaching and learning by focusing on the details and walking the corridors and playgrounds to ensure everything is as it should is really critical even in the most senior leader, Hutchinson says.

"It's the details that matter. Is the classroom tidy? Is the teacher's desk tidy, are they presenting a professional approach? All those things I think betray a mindset. The mindset is about high standards and it's manifested in all sorts of different ways. That to my mind is why the details matter. They are symptomatic of a set of standards. If students care about things it will be manifested in the detail. If teachers care they will be manifested in the detail as they want to go the extra mile."

A professional service

Llyn Codling, Executive Headteacher of Portswood and St Mary's Church of England primary schools in Southampton, believes passionately in the idea of teaching as a professional service.

"It's a huge thing for me. Teachers, and headteachers too, are servants. We are there for the children and we mustn't ever forget that. It's about being humble and being that servant who is there to make sure the learning and everything else is happening. It's why sometimes you have to have those courageous conversations with staff who are not teaching well. It doesn't mean they're easy and it doesn't mean there aren't times, however resilient you are, that you feel that you want to crawl under your desk and not come out for the rest of the day. It is about taking those deep breaths, being humble, being ready to serve, and remembering why you're doing it. Actually you are doing it for the children, and that's the greatest thing. At the end of the day, we are all there to support and lead the children."

In Codling's view, taking on executive responsibilities for several schools does not mean that a leader should lose contact with the children and parents they are there to serve. She is not one who believes that the title of 'headteacher' should be consigned to the history books.

"The heads I speak to that are really great heads never forget the children and the teaching. They are never afraid to roll up their sleeves and still go and teach and coach and walk the classrooms. I think sometimes the people who forget to do that – I don't think they don't want to, I think it's about forgetting why they're there. You always have to hang onto that about teaching, and what's important. I don't tend to go to heads' meetings, particularly if they are about health and safety and budgets. I've got other people who can go to those.

"It's about getting the right people on the bus. I've got a school business manager who's absolutely passionate about the budget and health and safety in buildings. She will do that side of it and she's on my school leadership team so she's very senior and she'll keep me informed. You don't have to do everything as a head and some people forget that. As a head you are a head teacher, not a head administrator, or head surveyor, or head accountant. My belief is if you lose that you do so at your peril, because you are losing your way.

"I'm head teacher and proud of that. I teach all the teachers in both my schools. There's a quote I'm fond of which is: 'I'm not a man, I'm not a woman, I'm not a person, I'm not myself, I am a teacher'. That's what it's about really."

One school's turn-around

In 2012, Alison Peacock, Headteacher at The Wroxham School in Potters Bar, Hertfordshire, co-authored a book called *Creating Learning without Limits* (Open University Press, 2012). It tells the story of how her school has created a learning environment that is 'inclusive, humane and enabling for everybody'. The book charts how the school, which was in special measures when she arrived in 2003, 'grew into a thriving community with distinctive views of learning, the curriculum and pedagogy'.

Peacock, who is also Network Leader and Associate Director of the Cambridge Primary Review, the independent enquiry into the future of primary education in England, is a passionate advocate of teachers exploring their own practice as a means of professional development. She also believes a headteacher's leadership qualities develop out of their qualities and experience as a classroom teacher.

"Increasingly I am doing a lot of work beyond the school and that's about a passion for saying education is really important for all children. That same vision that brought me into teaching in the first place is saying, 'Look, it doesn't have to be like this'. We don't have to have teachers who are feeling demoralised and trying to achieve inputs and targets and children who feel like they are widgets on a factory production line. We *can* have it all. We can have joyous education *and* high achievement.

"*Creating Learning without Limits* is a story about our school's turnaround and those dispositions for leadership within the school that are really key. They apply just as much to teachers working with children as to headteachers working with teachers. That kind of continuum around leadership works for all people at all stages. You don't take on the mantle of headship and suddenly have a new kind of skill set that arrives with it. It's a growing awareness of how we enable teams to work effectively."

A love of teaching

Mike Kent, one of the longest serving headteachers in Britain, with 31 years in post at Comber Grove Primary School in Camberwell, South London, believes a love of teaching and working with children are crucial qualities in a school leader.

"For a headteacher it's very easy to say, 'I've got so much paperwork today I can't talk to a child'. In Key Stage 2, I probably know the names of every child. I can tell you the things they are good at; the things they are not so good at, their backgrounds and a little bit about their general character. I think that's crucial. I tend to have a very high profile around the school. I'm not in my room very much. I still do a lot of teaching because I love it. That's what I am, a head teacher. I think any headteacher has got to have a love of teaching and still do it, if they can."

He is also a firm believer that headteachers should be able to demonstrate that they are excellent classroom teachers in order to set an example and earn the respect of their staff.

"It doesn't matter whether I go into the nursery and do some reading, or take an assembly, or bring things in and show the children, the teachers will be sitting there watching you. They will want to know that you're good at your trade. You get paid well for it so you should be able to do it at least as well as, and probably a lot better than, they can. It's really important to have that kind of respect with your staff.

The only way to be a good teacher is to keep doing it and sadly so many heads lose the skill because the further they get away from the classroom the less they want to do it. That's very sad. The joy of this job is teaching children. What you're doing as a headteacher is organising how that teaching is done and the experiences the children and staff can have in your school, but you are still basically a teacher. That's what we love doing."

4

Emotional intelligence

> **Successful school leaders are team-builders.
> They understand the importance of
> relationships, empower those around them and
> show great empathy.**

When Kenny Frederick took up the headship of George Green's School, a large comprehensive serving a disadvantaged multi-cultural community on the Isle of Dogs in Tower Hamlets, East London, in 1996, she knew she had a hard task ahead of her.

Relationships between the previous head, senior leadership, staff and governors had fractured and morale was at rock bottom. The extreme-right British National Party was active in the area and three years earlier had secured its first seat in local government on the local council. With ethnic tensions simmering and divisions among both the staff and pupils the school urgently needed a new sense of direction.

> "The racism was like nothing I have ever experienced. I really didn't understand what I'd taken on. I had worked in Hackney and Haringey all my life where there were very few white children, but we were always very anti-racist. I was quite shocked. There were tensions both within and outside the school. The staff were very strong working together. They supported each other but

often against the management. There were real divisions among the children. They didn't know each other. I remember walking around the school and noticing that the pupils weren't mixing. In the classrooms, all the white kids sat together, all the Bengali kids sat together. They didn't know each other's names. The previous head seemed to have a policy of, 'If I don't talk about it then it doesn't exist'."

Drawing people together

Frederick concedes now that she came to the job – her first headship – "as a bit of an innocent" and had little time to prepare for the interview.

"I remember being asked all sorts of questions about a prayer room and I hadn't realised there were arguments going on about whether the school should have a prayer room or not. Because I didn't have time I didn't do lots of research into the school. I had no sort of strategy other than to be myself. I think they must have been looking for someone who was a people person who could draw people together, which is why I got the job."

Her strategy proved to be somewhat revolutionary as she set about introducing an 'open door' policy for the school. In doing so she became one of the pioneers of a leadership style that is now common in British education but was then comparatively rare.

> "I decided that there was no model for the headteacher I wanted to be. I'd seen various ones in my time and the only person I knew how to be was me. For me, the job has always been about inclusion, about including everybody, starting with the staff.
>
> "So the first thing I set out to do was to mend relationships. I think people found it quite strange, the idea that my door was always open so that everybody could just drift in and talk to me. I remember my first day and people would come in and ask me all sorts of strange questions about boilers and other things I didn't have a clue about and I just said, 'I don't know, what do you think?' I was always quite happy to say to people if I didn't know, and then take their advice which I think they appreciated."

This approach is an acknowledgement that school leaders, although responsible for major decision-making and providing strategic direction for their institutions, do not have to pretend to be the fonts of all knowledge and wisdom. Simply by throwing back a question at:

- a member of staff
- a pupil
- a parent
- a member of the governing body,

a leader is inviting them to contribute their view, share their expertise and, potentially, solve a problem.

"I think it's really important. The worst thing you can do is try to blag it and pretend you are the expert on everything. Clearly you are not and you'll get found out. People appreciate that. You bring people in, find out what their expertise is and you thank them for it and recognise what they do publicly and not pretend it's all your own work. I can't be anybody other than myself and I think that's stood me in good stead," says Frederick.

Building the right team

For many heads the importance of getting relationships right is crucial to achieving their overall vision and ambitions for their schools. That means developing good relations between:

- the leadership team
- the staff
- the pupils
- the parents
- the wider community.

This process is tied in with the values headteachers want to instil. The key to this is building the right team. Putting the right team in place enables a school to perform at its best and create a shared vision.

Simply appointing the right people to the right posts is not enough, however. The best headteachers are keen to delegate responsibilities and believe in empowering their staff. This process is often called 'distributed leadership' but the most successful school leaders go far beyond the jargon. What glues these relationships together is the great empathy these leaders have for the feelings and concerns of others. This requires the ability and readiness to listen to the concerns of staff and the wider community and appreciate why they sometimes find it hard to accept a particular vision and desire for change. The best heads are sensitive, sympathetic and understanding. They are good at listening to people's problems and finding ways to resolve them. Having a great team around them which shares a common sense of purpose greatly helps with this process.

Emotional intelligence

A good name for this crucial quality is 'the people gene'. It is a quality that has become widely known as 'emotional intelligence' and is increasingly seen as a key leadership skill by global businesses when recruiting top executives. Daniel Goleman, author of the influential book *Emotional Intelligence* (Bantam, 1995) identifies it as having five components:

- self-awareness
- self-regulation
- motivation
- empathy
- social skill.

Taken together, Goleman argues in a subsequent article in the *Harvard Business Review* (1998), these attributes are more important for successful leadership than other traditional leadership traits such as general intelligence, toughness, determination and vision. Describing emotional intelligence as "the *sine qua non* of leadership" he says: "Without it, a person can have the best training in the world, an incisive, analytical mind, and an endless supply of smart ideas, but he still won't make a great leader".

Kenny Frederick believes the business of running an effective school is "all about emotional intelligence". Underpinning her open and inclusive style of leadership is an awareness of her own strengths and weaknesses and the confidence to acknowledge them to others.

"People appreciate honesty. I am far from perfect and they know that. People actually appreciate that you are not trying to pretend anything. I have a well-known problem with apostrophes but I will always get somebody to check them for me. I have other strengths to bring to the table and people appreciate that. That's why you have to have a good team about you and I think I have a brilliant team with all sorts of different strengths. They love to use those strengths and they are very proud of that. It's important to make sure you don't appoint people who are all exactly like you."

Including the whole staff

As a new headteacher, Frederick set about creating the sort of open and inclusive structures she believed were needed to heal the divisions within the school. Not only was this about creating a new management style, it was also about bringing in new ideas and expertise and including the whole staff in discussions affecting the school's future.

"When I started off it was a very small leadership team with three deputy heads. They were used to working in that particular way. One of the first things I did was to appoint a senior finance person because I'm no good at finances and I felt it was very important to have someone with that skill on my leadership team. I brought two members of the support staff onto the leadership team which wasn't popular with two of my deputies, but they had to put up with it. Also I appointed one of the middle leaders to a senior teacher post for a while to come onto the team to give them experience and to help them develop. So it was a bigger team.

"Previously, leadership had always been something that went on behind closed doors. People didn't know what the head or the deputy got up to. You were just told off by them occasionally. I wanted to demystify headship which is why I had an open-door system and also a policy of bringing members of the middle leadership onto the senior team. They bring in a different perspective but also it demystifies things and helps people to see the big picture.

"The other thing I introduced immediately was performance management for support staff because they hadn't had any development. Right from the first day I said that training must be for all staff not just for teachers. My belief is that if you include the staff they will include the youngsters and so it was all about the language we used when talking about staff and children in order to show we were all part of the team.

"I would get very cross if I was walking down the corridor and people walked past and didn't say hello. I would say to staff, 'You acknowledge and say hello, good morning, how are you doing' or whatever, to kids, adults or whoever it is. I've never wanted school to be a cold, unemotional institution. I wanted it to be warm so that people can approach you and talk to you. It's also important the way staff treat each other, the language they use with each other. I remember going on a course once about homophobia and someone said the kids learn often from the way we behave towards each other as adults and I think that's so true. We have to be role models and show that we respect each other and respect the children."

A roller-coaster ride

Running what she describes as "a truly inclusive school" in an area that has one of the highest child poverty rates in Britain has been a roller-coaster ride. Ofsted, in its first inspection report after her appointment as Principal, described it as an improving school and, in 2005, rated it as "a good school with many very good and excellent features". Frederick's leadership was rated as excellent. In 2008, however, a disappointing set of GCSE results was followed by a 'notice to improve' from Ofsted. Instead of walking away, Frederick responded with plans to radically revamp the curriculum, introducing the International Baccalaureate diploma in the sixth form. It became one of the most rapidly improved schools in London, almost doubling the proportion of pupils achieving five GCSE A*–C grades, including English and mathematics, between 2008 and 2012.

When the school was re-inspected in the spring of 2013 it received an overall "good" grading by Ofsted. Inspectors praised the leadership team for their "determined and relentless focus on improving teaching and achievement". This, the inspectors noted in their inspection report, was "driven by a passionate belief that all students, irrespective of their circumstances, are entitled to the best possible education". Tellingly, the report reserves its greatest praise for the school's provision for students' spiritual, moral, social and cultural development which it describes as the most significant strength of the school. "Students demonstrate considerable respect for students from different religious and ethnic backgrounds," the report says.

As Frederick describes it, George Green's is now very different to the racially divided and dysfunctional school she inherited in 1996.

"It's a very humane institution. The staff really care about the pupils, they care about each other. Some people would perhaps say that's got in the way of results sometimes but I don't see that. It's giving pupils the confidence to learn. Some of the kids have terrible things to deal with in their lives and I think we've helped them to develop their own resilience. You can't necessarily change children's lives but you can change the way that they deal with things and I think we've been able to show them that you can get through terrible times.

"We are a very emotional school. If somebody dies or someone is ill staff will cry. Kids need to see that, they need to see the whole spectrum of human ways of behaving. What a lot of them see out on the street and at home is a violent, aggressive form of behaviour and don't know any other way to handle it other than to hit out. My aim has always been to try to show them that there's a different way, which is why we do conflict resolutions and why we try to talk things out and do a lot of work on empathy. For a lot of them that's not a normal part of their upbringing. For me, it has always been about developing the whole person not just preparing them for GCSEs."

Relationships and values

Roger Pope, Principal of Kingsbridge Community College in Devon, believes that relationships matter more than anything else when it comes to establishing a happy and successful school. One reason they are so important, he says, is that they are closely linked with values.

"Get the relationships right – open, trusting, humorous – and much else follows naturally. People feel motivated. They want to follow you. They want to do their best for you. It is tied with values because it is part of living what you are trying to model for students. It would be odd to be claiming to educate kids to be good citizens if you do not model those values in your everyday dealings with people. I also think work plays a big part in people's lives and that a head therefore has a moral duty to make work as enjoyable and fulfilling as possible."

Pope acknowledges that there are many successful school leaders who would put relationships much lower down their list of priorities because they work more through authoritative systems. But if you want to get the best out of your staff you have to build good, trusting relationships, he believes.

"It's about institutional trust. If you build high levels of institutional trust then it means you get a lot more done a lot more quickly, because you're not wasting time having to discuss every small thing you're doing with umpteen different unions. You do not have to persuade people to do things. You suggest something, they will subject it to suitable scrutiny and generally speaking they will go with you. Relationships lie at the heart of it for that reason."

For Teresa Tunnadine, Headteacher of The Compton School in North London, the opportunity to build relationships and the daily interactions with staff, pupils and other people associated with school life is one of the joys of the job.

"A lot of heads will say, 'It's very lonely, I'm the one that's ultimately making decisions' but I have to say I don't feel like that at all. I have got a very big senior team of 11 and that's partly because I do a lot of system leadership work, working at the Department for Education or the National College or working in other schools, supporting other heads, mentoring new heads. So the team that I have gathered around me are amazing. Each of them is much better at what they do than I would be if I were doing their job, and they're very different. It's a team of all talents who work very well together.

"It doesn't mean we agree with each other all the time but there is the space to disagree. About three or four years ago I reorganised them and, to use the analogy, put them on the right seats on the bus [the analogy comes from Jim Collins's book, *Good to Great* (Random House, 2001)]. Some of them were in the wrong seats and weren't as comfortable. I've now moved them – with their agreement and with discussion and negotiation – into the jobs they are now flying at. It is so satisfying to see people grow. All of them have come through the system and came to the school as a NQT or as a new middle leader and when you see them doing the work they are doing now it's so satisfying. For me part of the joy of doing the job is watching people grow. I have mentored a number of new heads and again seeing them grow and develop to the point where I don't need to be there any more is hugely satisfying."

Mutual trust

Like Pope, she believes an essential part of building up a strong team which bonds together is creating a sense of mutual trust.

"It's very important as a leader to be calm and measured and not to make snap decisions unless you need to. You need to show consistency and fairness. When people ask for time off, there has to be the feeling that you don't have favourites. There has to be a sense that 'It is the same for me as it is for them' and that there is a kind of reasonableness and clarity about the decisions that are made. You also need to show that you are listening and reacting to what other people are saying. All of that is very important.

"We have had Investors in People in recently. They interviewed 50 staff and all of them said that is what they get here: the sense that there is a reasoned approach, fairness, and an open-door policy. It is a very special place. It is about relationships. That doesn't mean we don't have tough conversations, but I think we are at a point where we can have those tough conversations and people know it is professional not personal. It goes back to the moral purpose; it's about making it better for the children that we've got here."

Talent-spotting

Another important aspect of building effective teams is having the ability to spot talent and enable people to grow and take on extra responsibility and bigger jobs, says Tunnadine.

"We are always spotting talent. We are looking at people who join us and seeing who the future stars are going to be. We have got a lot of them here and we provide them with opportunities as soon as possible – during their first year or into their second year, we provide bursaries so that they can begin to take responsibility and we give a lot of decision-making and responsibility out to middle leaders so they can run their departments in the way they see fit. It's about trusting people and delegating responsibility with a lot of support and training, to enable people to be the very best at their job."

There is a strong nurturing aspect to this strand of leadership. Many successful headteachers, supported by national organisations such as the National College and the charity Future Leaders, speak of the importance of growing and developing talented teachers and middle leaders and encouraging them to take on senior roles. But there is also an element of 'tough love' or 'tough empathy' involved in weeding out people who do not fit in or who actively undermine teams. It also means being able to recognise when to put pressure on a member of staff to raise their performance and when to lend a helping hand. Dame Joan McVittie, Headteacher of Woodside High School in North London, puts it this way:

> "I've worked with a number of people over the years that really had low levels of emotional intelligence and they can totally destroy teams – and whole schools actually. I think it's absolutely critical to be able to recognise that. It's about knowing which members of staff you need to put pressure on and which members of staff put sufficient pressure on themselves. I've actually seen some members of my own team make quite serious errors and I have had to pull them in and say, 'Do not come down hard on that particular member of staff because they are already very hard on themselves. It's this one here, who's lazy, that you need to keep the pressure on'. I always thought that was something you could teach leaders but I'm now beginning to think that it's not. I think emotional intelligence is instinctive."

The school as a team

Patricia Scott, Headteacher of St Luke's High School in Barrhead, East Renfrewshire, Scotland, believes that an essential element of any successful school is the strength of relationships and the care and concern staff and pupils have for one another.

> "I think that is an absolutely key building block and we don't get anywhere if we don't have that. It's about creating that whole sense of a school as a team and one that everyone respects. It's not about taking orders. The whole machine doesn't work unless everyone has an investment in it and everyone cares about one another. We come to work as people and we have everything that goes along in everyone's normal life as part of that as well.
>
> "The whole ethos of a health-promoting school as we are is one that I've been very signed up to for a very long time. It's about supporting the health and well-being of everyone in the school. If we can assure that health and well-being to the best of our ability then people will be able to teach better, youngsters will be able to learn better, support staff will be able to support them better, and so on. There has to be a real sense that this is our school, that we care about one another and we're trying to do our best."

Scott believes that creating the right supportive environment is a prerequisite for any successful school and that you can only challenge staff and pupils to perform at their best if you care about them as individuals.

"If people are well-cared-for and have that structure round about them then you get much, much more out of people. People are not numbers in a book, they don't simply come into school to teach and go away again. I think it's really, really important to have that investment in the school and that care for the whole community. It is actually what breeds success, because if people have that investment they want to do the best by themselves and by everyone else in the school."

Alison Peacock, Headteacher of The Wroxham School in Potters Bar, Hertfordshire, is another leader who rejects the traditional notion that being the head of a school is a lonely occupation.

"I have never once as a headteacher sat in my room and felt lonely. When you do an NPQH and they talk about the loneliness of headship I can honestly say I have never had one single day when I have felt lonely as a headteacher. And that's because I've never set myself up as someone who knows all the answers. As soon as you do then you are going to be lonely because nobody knows all the answers. It's about leading a team where everyone can contribute and that's hugely empowering."

She believes the ability to understand and empathise with children – an essential skill for classroom teachers – is equally important for senior school leaders.

"I think one of the things that's really important whenever you are working with a group of children is that, instead of saying what's wrong with the child if he or she is unable to work in the way you hope they might be able to, it's about saying, 'What else can I do differently to find a way through for that child?' The same principle is there when it comes to working with staff, parents or anybody else in the community. If there isn't a relationship of trust and if people aren't communicating with you, the tempting thing is to say, 'These are hard to reach parents', or 'This is a member of staff that needs to go onto capability'. Sometimes it's about thinking, 'What can I do differently to enable that colleague to engage in a more fruitful way?'

"That's not to say that sometimes there doesn't have to be a tough edge because that's another strand of leadership. You do have to be able at some point to say, 'I have to be the advocate for the children'. So if it's a member of staff or a parent who is behaving in a way that I think is endangering the children, or is disrespectful, or is damaging the culture in which we are trying to work then I have to be strong enough to challenge that. But while doing that I still ask, 'Why are they doing this in the first place?'"

Making time to listen

School leaders also need to make time to listen in order to build trusting relationships, says Peacock. This is not always an easy thing to do when there are so many pressures and demands competing for heads' attention but can often resolve problems and make a school stronger.

"That's really key. If you just wade in, if you are tempted to be solution-focused all the time, you might be trying to solve the wrong problem. Unless you really listen then actually, what is first said might be masking the real issue which might only emerge when a person's got their hand on the door handle and they're about to leave the room. Then you think, 'Ah, that's what this is really about'. But unless you listen, you might never get there.

"There is so much pressure associated with the job that sometimes giving time and space to sit back and listen, feels like a luxury, as opposed to a necessity, but I think it is a necessity. It's the same with the children. When I came to The Wroxham behaviour was a real challenge on the playground. And one of the very first things that I started doing was providing children with time to calm down and to write their side of the story and talk individually about what had happened. For them, that had never happened before. No one had ever listened to their side of the story. The same is true of anybody really. You either leap in and say 'I've already decided this, I haven't got time to talk to you now', or you listen. Often, if you can give that space then things that would otherwise build into something much bigger and take much longer to unravel don't become tangled up in the first place."

Andrew Fleck, Headmaster of Sedbergh School in Cumbria, believes that being able to show empathy with the many different people that school leaders come into contact with in the course of their job is "the most important 'soft skill'". It is essential to be able to understand their situation and respond appropriately. By doing so a leader can:

- defuse crises
- build relationships

- inspire achievement
- generate loyalty.

Like Peacock, he also stresses the importance of listening.

"Most people who work in schools are idealistic and therefore it's important to be able to tap into the vocational aspects of the teaching staff and being able to liberate their ambitions. We can't do that as headteachers if we simply look at the role as delivering lessons. It becomes a mechanical process. I spend a lot of my time simply listening to people, but also in coaching middle managers and younger staff in how to manage situations and resolving problems. It's about both demonstrating an emotional awareness of my staff and coaching them to treat and manage each other in an emotionally sensitive way. We are constantly dealing with parents and pupils and all manner of human interactions.

"Another critical part of what I do is to be able to change from business negotiation – which still requires emotional intelligence and empathy but can be quite tough – to the father of the 15-year-old girl who has discovered that she is self-harming, or the teacher whose wife has just been diagnosed with cancer. Or the housemaster's wife who has had an accident involving a motor bike and the motor bike rider is killed. The whole human condition runs through my office and I have to be able to change at the drop of the hat. You get no warning."

This ability to show emotional intelligence comes partly with experience and is something that anyone who wants to be successful as a school leader needs to work on and develop, says Fleck.

"I don't think it's solely instinctive. Learning is probably my strongest skill. I am always learning. I remember once a very senior woman chief executive making the point that the more elevated the position you are in the softer, gentler, more empathic the manager-leader needs to be. Those skills become more critical as you progress through your career. The reason is that your position gives you the authority so you don't need to be tough. It's counter-intuitive. It's how you make yourself available to people."

Using intuition

Madeleine Vigar is Principal of The Castle Partnership Academy Trust, which provides all-through learning at Castle Manor Academy and Place Farm Primary Academy in Haverhill, Suffolk. She says she learned to rely on emotional intelligence, which she equates to intuition, as a young teacher when she took a course called Counselling Aspects in Education at the Tavistock Institute in North London. It is something she developed as a classroom teacher and now uses extensively as a school leader.

"We call it here, 'keeping your antennae out'. It's about being able to read people's non-verbal signs, being able to read their eye contact because quite often that will tell you a lot. Sometimes I have to physically make myself sit back and watch people because just by observing the way people are can tell you so much. If you read those signs well then you know how to create the right conditions for your staff or the right conditions in the classroom. It's important because it enables you to improve things for people. It can also enable you to pre-empt things. The whole skill of leadership is about being able to pre-empt something that might happen next."

As an example she cites an occasion when she was coming out of a leadership team meeting and noticed a parent anxiously standing in reception.

"We were about to have an Ofsted inspector come in the door and this parent had a slight look on her face. I was able to say to my leadership team, 'Just check that parent is all right will you?' What I didn't want was her suddenly jumping up and down in front of the Ofsted inspector. If you can pre-empt a potentially difficult situation just by checking someone is OK, by having some emotional awareness, you can save yourself a lot of trouble."

Staff coaching

Catherine Paine, Executive Headteacher of Mount Street Academy and Saxilby Church of England Primary School in Lincolnshire, believes that the best way to build a successful team is to act as a coach to your staff, constantly urging them to go "harder, faster, stronger". This leadership model, drawn from the world of professional sport, is strongly linked with her desire to inspire pupils and staff in her schools (in the words of the late Steve Jobs, co-founder of Apple), "to do great work and love what you do".

After becoming one of the youngest headteachers in the country at the age of 28, in 1998, Paine has been the substantive head of three schools and became a National Leader of Education in 2011, advising other primary heads on leadership issues. Mount Street, which has 300 children aged three to seven on its rolls, was graded as 'outstanding' by Ofsted in 2010 and went on to become one of the country's first primary academies. As executive leader of two schools she has recognised the impossibility of attempting to be a personal coach to everybody and has introduced a line-management system so that the coaching filters down to every level.

"I strongly believe in making sure that there are key people who will act as coaches to others. So we have a structure where everybody is line-managed, either six-weekly, three-weekly or two-weekly. That filters its way up to me and I line-manage personally the heads of school, SENCOs and the school business director who are on two-weekly line-management. I am not line-managed but have a professional coach in London who I see four or five times a year who is about five years further on in his career than I am. He's a National Leader of Education and works for the Department for Education. So I also have challenge.

"Everybody within the structure has got somebody who is saying 'harder, faster, stronger', and for each member of staff there's a report that makes its way back up the structure to me. So there's a coaching model in place that's all about our drive for excellence and I think that capacity building has been pivotal in enabling us to be effective. There are too many headteachers who are just going under because they are keeping too much to themselves. What I have had to do is to build the capacity for myself to be out of the equation quite a lot of the time but to also know that coaching model is still going on in my absence."

Ani Magill, Headteacher of St John the Baptist School, a high-achieving Catholic comprehensive in Woking, Surrey, also believes strongly in using coaching to develop people.

"The coaching model is definitely how we operate here. There's nothing top down; we use the Jacuzzi method, not the hosepipe method. We're there underneath, quietly supporting and making people feel good, not standing them up against the wall and hosing them down and telling them this is how you do it. It takes more time to coach and develop people but it definitely gets medium and long term gains," she says.

Developing school leaders

Developing people as leaders is something Magill feels passionately about. As an experienced headteacher with a track record of turning around schools that have got into difficulty, her school is a designated National Training School and she works extensively mentoring new heads and other school leaders.

One of the key features of her school is a ten-point model setting out what Magill considers to be the outstanding features of successful leadership. This stresses the importance of leading by example, developing others and the need to reflect on and evaluate performance. It also highlights the importance of personal qualities such as humility, integrity and positivity (Appendix 3, see page 168).

"One of the very big parts of our work here is to identify and grow and develop leaders for the future at all levels. So we have leadership programmes at every level from newly qualified teachers upwards. Our modus operandi is to lead by serving others. It's about serving other people, inspiring other people, taking care of other people, looking after them, and developing them so they do the best they possibly can. There is a quote ["Opportunities for success increase exponentially by the number of leaders you create within your organisation", Dr Frank Rudnesky of Widener University, USA, and author of 50 Great Things Leaders Do (lulu.com, 2011)] – that you 'measure leadership, not by the number of people you've led, but by the number of leaders you've created'. At least 18 staff that I have worked with have gone on to headship and very successfully as well.

"People come here to work and I say to them, 'I want you to stay for three years, and we guarantee we'll get you ready for the next level'. That's part of the deal. We expect 100 per cent from people but we will get them ready for the next level. At the end of the day we believe that leading people means we serve them, so the job of the leadership team is to serve the teachers."

Developing school leaders has been the core responsibility of the National College for School Leadership since it was established by Tony Blair's Labour government in 2000. Maggie Farrar, the College's Executive Director and Interim Chief Executive in the run-up to its merger with the Teaching Agency in April 2013, denies the charge from critics that it has tended to promote a uniform style of leadership in the past.

> "If we put store by anything we put quite a lot of store by distributed leadership. Sometimes when a leader goes in to take over a failing school you can't start a distributed model immediately. If that's never been prevalent in the school, if there are an awful lot of systems, structures, processes and procedures to get right very quickly, you might have to have a much more directive, pace-setting style of leadership. But no leader can keep that up forever and any leader who does that and doesn't have a distributed leadership style will never leave a legacy. It's important for leaders to be able to lead sustainable change and leave a legacy. That can be measured by the number of other leaders that leader grows and how distributed the leadership is in their school."

A personal leadership style

Developing a personal leadership style can be a tricky thing to do for aspirant headteachers and principals. In many cases it is a question of being true to oneself; of doing the job with openness, honesty and integrity, but also with a clear sense of purpose and a determination to succeed.

Lynn Slinger, Headteacher of Forest Way Special School in Coalville, Leicestershire, believes other factors can also come into play. She cites her own background growing up on a Sheffield council estate and being a parent herself as examples of how personal circumstances have helped her to understand and empathise with pupils, parents and staff members who may be struggling and need support and guidance.

> "Perhaps because I'm from Sheffield I have been stereotyped as a blunt northerner. I do call a spade a spade, though whether that's because I'm from the north or whether it's just my character, I don't know. But I do think people skills are really important and looking at different leaders I've met through my career their interpersonal skills really do vary. I don't know how without emotional intelligence you can function as a school leader. I suppose there are some that are successful, though they would have to build a team around them that can fill in the gaps. But I think to be a really inspirational leader you do need that."

Like Maggie Farrar, Slinger believes a great leader needs to be able to adapt their approach according to the immediate demands of the job.

> "It depends on the stage of a school's life. In 18 years of headship I've been a total autocrat and I've been a total democrat. It's depended on who I'm working with, what needs doing and at what stage in its development the organisation is at. It's about using a range of styles and your staff knowing you will use a range of styles. So even if you've got a very democratic way of working, ultimately if something has to be done you might have to be quite autocratic and say, 'Sorry, I've got to take this decision. I'm the head and I am accountable. We need to do this even if the majority of you don't want it.' I will delegate but when I do delegate, initially I will still keep an eye on things to try and coach people. If you delegate things and take your eye off the ball you can end up in real trouble. Certainly when I first came to this school I was a total autocrat."

Sue Hargadon, Principal of Farlingaye High School in Suffolk, also believes successful delegation requires total trust on the part of the headteacher. That is something that comes gradually through coaching people and watching them grow into their various roles, she says.

"When I trust people I trust them implicitly. When I'm not sure about people I tend to be much more involved in what they're doing. Also, when someone is new I tend to put more time into that part of the school particularly on the senior leadership team. Last year for example, we had a new Upper School Co-ordinator so I did a lot of work with her, and then gradually as you get to know she's competent and very good then that's fine. My Deputy Head is just brilliant, but when he first came he constantly wanted to check things with me. Now I trust him implicitly."

Like many other successful leaders, Hargadon believes the team she has built is "the best in the world". The strength of any successful team, she believes, greatly depends on mutual trust and crucially that requires the headteacher or principal to be highly visible about the school and to lead by example. She also believes staff should be given recognition and rewards for taking on extra duties or project work. She always tries to "do little things like write to staff every Christmas – a personal message in a Christmas card. I always write and thank everybody for everything they do," she says.

In order to build a successful team a leader also needs to be able to read people well, recognise those with real talent and – crucially, when it comes to hiring staff – only accept the best.

"I think it's very important that I never appoint anybody who I don't think is good. Recently, I had to make four temporary appointments for a year, which caused us a nightmare to be quite frank because I couldn't get anybody good enough to fill the posts on a permanent basis. I would never appoint anybody who I don't think will be good. I would never do the 'Oh my God, it's June and we need to appoint someone' scenario. So I've always got people that I think are worth working with," says Hargadon.

Her determination not to put up with second best shows the importance of having great 'people skills', but also that emotional intelligence needs to be deployed alongside other key leadership traits, such as determination and the courage to make the right decision. One of the most important, and hardest to master, is judgement.

5

Judgement

Successful school leaders show great judgement. They make the right calls and are wise leaders.

Joan McVittie has spent much of her career working in some of London's most challenging secondary schools. In 2006, she took on one of her biggest challenges when she was appointed Headteacher of White Hart Lane School in Haringey, which had been languishing at the bottom of the capital's league tables with just 17 per cent of pupils gaining five GCSE grades A*–C. Within five years, she had transformed the school's fortunes, dramatically improving results and, under its new name of Woodside High School, it received an outstanding grading from Ofsted in 2011.

Recognising potential

Yet her career path might have been very different had it not been for the judgement of one man, who recognised her potential and set her on a course to become one of the most notable 'turnaround' heads in the country.

"I was working part-time in an independent school. It suited me. I suppose you could call me a corporate wife. I had three young children and I had a husband with a very high-powered job and we tended to move round the country. My husband was made redundant and he said, 'Oh, we will not be able to afford our lifestyle'; so I thought OK, I'll just have to step up. There was a job for a senior leader – it was senior mistress, actually in those days – in St Bonaventure's in Newham, and the Headteacher was Michael Wilshaw.

"Mike's a great risk-taker and he obviously looked at me and saw great potential. I basically jumped from being Head of Biology in a small independent school to being a senior mistress in a large boys' comprehensive. He put me in charge of assessment at Key Stage 4 and then the person in charge of assessment at Key Stage 3 broke his ankle and was off for a year, so I was put in charge of assessment for the whole school. He also put me in charge of the budget. And that was it. As I said, Mike is a real risk-taker and he will give you a free rein as long as you get the right outcomes, and that was where I learned absolutely loads about leadership."

McVittie is quick to acknowledge the debt she owes Sir Michael Wilshaw, who would go on to become the founding Principal of one of England's first and most successful state-funded academies, Mossbourne Academy in Hackney, East London. In January 2012 he was appointed Chief Inspector of Schools for England and Head of Ofsted.

"I owe Mike a lot. I went back to work for him another time. I had gone off to a deputy headship in another London school and then one day Eastleigh School in Newham was put in special measures and the local authority asked Mike to go in and take charge. He needed a deputy to go in with him and he contacted me, so I joined him. It was 1998. We worked there for a year together to get the school out of special measures. At the end of it he got a knighthood and I went on to a headship."

McVittie, who herself was made a Dame in the New Year's Honours list 2013, describes Wilshaw as a quintessential risk-taker and a keen judge of people's character.

"He has an amazing skill in judging who will make not just a good teacher but an exceptional teacher. He really seems to know who will make the best teacher for the children. He will take risks. Who else in the country would have taken a middle-aged woman with children just about to start secondary school who had worked part-time in a small Catholic independent school as a biology teacher? Who else on this earth would have gone, 'That woman will do me for a senior teacher'. But he did."

Taking risks

Having the confidence to take risks is a key skill displayed by many successful leaders. Lynn Slinger recalls one of the first decisions she had to make after taking up the Headship of Forest Way Special School in Coalville, Leicestershire, in the mid-1990s. Her vision was to make Forest Way the best special school in the country and a centre for excellence, an ambitious aspiration for a relatively small school in a former mining community. The school had a reputation for caring for its pupils, but Slinger wanted to strengthen the leadership and focus on attainment.

"I took a real risk. I needed a good deputy head and I had a supply teacher who was totally unproven in any management position and I appointed her as the Deputy Head. It caused massive unrest. She was on a massive learning curve but I saw that her work ethic and her ideals were very similar to mine. I knew that in partnership with her, and the way the governors wanted to move the school forward, we could do the job together. She's still with me 17 years later and she's proved that. It was a big risk that I took but it paid off."

While risk-taking can bring enormous benefits, however, it is not simply a matter of having large ambitions, taking a deep breath and diving in. Even the most confident heads need to be able to weigh up decisions and make a balanced judgement. To do this effectively a leader needs to be able to think clearly about what is important and what is not, and act accordingly.

"I do think that in any job, headship particularly, there are so many conflicting interests, so many different things going on, so many different people, that sometimes it's really hard to be clear about things," says Slinger.

"The amount of paperwork is unbelievably massive and the bureaucracy can really muddle things. So I think having that clarity, and being able to cut through some of this stuff that gets in the way is a real attribute that leaders need. I have seen people as leaders not cope very well because they can't see the wood for the trees and they get in a mess with all this stuff we have to deal with. They are quite good in other ways but they can't always see what's important."

Leaders need to be well organised, able to choose between competing priorities and to focus on the 'big picture'. But they also need to be able to marshal all the available evidence and use their experience in order to make balanced judgements.

"Sometimes when I work with new heads the biggest bear trap they fall into is not-knowing what they don't know. They are clear about what they think should happen but their lack of experience can make them take the wrong decision that could cause massive problems. It's important to have that clarity, but you also need to be able to weigh up different scenarios. You can be very clear about what you think should happen but you also need to be sure it's a balanced view and that you aren't focusing on the wrong things," Slinger says.

Making the right judgement for a school

The ability to make big decisions about the future direction of a school requires boldness in a leader. But equally he or she needs the emotional intelligence to be able to judge whether they are making the right decision when faced with a particular set of circumstances, in a particular context. Andrew Hutchinson, Executive Principal of Parkside Federation Academies in Cambridge, describes this attribute as "gut feeling". It is something he relied on when he took charge of the neighbouring Coleridge Community College in Cambridge, then in special measures, in 2005.

> "When you take on a new school you need to be aware of where you are going, what the impact is that you are having on the people around you and what will work and what won't – what you can achieve and what you can't achieve. There are things that you would like potentially to do or might work, but you just know they just won't have any traction with the people you're working with. It would just be a solution that wouldn't work.
>
> "A lot of people who take over schools like Coleridge go in for a strong blazer and tie culture. One of the models for school improvement is a strong uniform policy, zero tolerance and all the rest of it. That wasn't what we did with Coleridge. We treated students at Coleridge in the same way as historically the students at Parkside have been treated, with a liberal but demanding ethos. That has worked. It was about being true to the conviction that it would ultimately deliver better outcomes than a more draconian approach.
>
> "I think we've been justified in that. We've seen students develop in the way that we want them to develop, and which is analogous to the way the students at Parkside have behaved. It was a case of understanding that that was what we wanted to achieve; it was what the staff wanted and the students wanted rather than taking a more confrontational approach. Our approach has been that we wanted to allow people to be educated rather than coerce them into certain patterns of behaviour. That has always been the Parkside ethos."

Developing a particular vision for a school inevitably involves key judgements about the strategic direction it should take. Hutchinson wanted to create an ethos based on partnership and student engagement.

"We often underestimate that ethos and culture are at root at least partly created by the students. A lot of the school improvement models ignore that. They're about strong management and leadership and are often a top-down model. That can work in terms of a quick fix. A strongly managed community is clearly better than an anarchic one. But to move beyond that, if you want to take your school on a journey to be outstanding, you have got to have students as partners in that journey. You can't do any better than be a good school unless the students are active partners and subscribe to the view of what the school needs to be. A crucial part of the head's job is to ensure that the students are shaping the vision for the school. They are the ones that leave that legacy for the younger ones; they're the ones that really do create the culture. But they don't create it in their own right; they need to be taught how to create a culture. That's our job."

A crucial part of this shaping process is a leader's ability to make the right judgements. This involves a complex mixture of instinct, experience, self-awareness and being honest enough to acknowledge and correct one's own mistakes.

"Even from day one you have to have an instinct for what's wrong. Your gut feeling has to be a good one if you are to be effective," says Hutchinson.

"As you go on you learn things and your judgements become better because they become informed by experience and practice. As a head you make mistakes at all stages and continue to make mistakes. Part of the ability to make good judgements is being able to judge when you've got it wrong, to admit that you've got it wrong, and to change things. That is absolutely crucial. The ability to recognise that your judgement isn't always right is equally as important as having that strong sense of getting it right. But you shouldn't be afraid of making judgements. If you don't take the risks and you only ever make judgements you think are safe judgements then in the end the organisation that you lead will be a poorer place."

Capacity to lead change

Geoff Barton, Headteacher of King Edward VI School in Bury St Edmunds, Suffolk, believes a key measure of leadership is the capacity to lead change. This requires both the courage to take bold and decisive action when required but also the ability to make constant small adjustments, or tweaks, in order to make the organisation function at full capacity.

"You have to be able to make a judgement about things. What sometimes happens is that people put too much emphasis on experience. I think that experience is less important than the ability to make the right judgements. It seems to me that there are some changes that are worth doing and some that are probably worth leaving and it's a question of deciding which ones to prioritise. For example, we moved six years ago to a three-period day, with long lessons, and then turned all the bells off. We decided to do that because I was walking around the school with my deputy one day, and he said: 'Look in every classroom, Geoff, and what you'll see is the great strength of this school, teachers love teaching'. And so I said, 'What do you think their weakness is?' And he said, 'Teachers love teaching'.

"The problem is they over-teach. They talk too much and however much you ask them to do less, the only way to get them to do that is by changing to long lessons. It seemed to me that this was a key change the school needed because it was going to change teachers' behaviour, lead to an emphasis on planning and then on pace and variety in lessons, and it seemed to me that was a really good decision. At the time it was pretty controversial with some departments, who thought that it was going to be a disaster. Some students felt it would be boring and some parents thought it was unthinkable. But when we introduced it, 95 per cent of staff, parents and students really liked it.

"The interesting thing I learnt about doing that is that the reason we *could* change something that was in one sense fundamental to the school, was because on my first day when I started as a new head [in 2002] we had changed little things. We changed the school website, the school newsletter and we smartened up the school uniform straight away. All of them were cosmetic changes, but they sent out a message that the school was under new management.

"Tweaking small things can show you have an appetite for changing things. Sometimes you miss your moment. I was advised to spend my first term as a head just getting under the skin of the school, looking at what needed to change and in a sense I did do that. But the risk is that in seeming not to change anything at all you can seem like you are someone who isn't going to change anything and you lose your honeymoon period.

"I remember on the first day saying to staff we're going to stop children wearing trainers – any child wearing them will not go into lessons. Someone said, 'You can't do that, this is a town school'. But we bought a load of plimsolls and we wrote to parents to say if their child comes to school in trainers they will be given plimsolls at the school gate and if they refused to wear them they wouldn't be going into lessons. And it just disappeared. It's superficial in one sense, but it did show the symbolism of change."

The art of good judgement

While judgement undoubtedly improves with experience even the most seasoned leader gets things wrong. Successful heads have the ability to recognise the need to change and adapt their organisations and are constantly searching for ways to improve. Roger Pope, Principal of Kingsbridge Community College in Devon, believes no school leader ever perfects the art of good judgement.

"I think you never fully achieve it. I once talked to a head about his staff and he said 'I've been here long enough so that I've appointed all the staff and they're all great'. And I thought 'you pompous, arrogant twit!' No matter how long you do things, you still get it wrong. It doesn't necessarily need to be intuitive, but I think you need to be of a reflective and humble disposition. What then happens is that when you do get things wrong, you learn from it and you try not to make the same mistakes again," he says.

"I would say I have learnt leadership by being a leader really. You don't learn leadership from textbooks. You learn it by doing it and by seeing what it is that motivates and what upsets people; and reflecting on that, trying not to do it again, and being very intuitive and sensitive. I think one of the things we do very well here at Kingsbridge is that we are very sensitive to the shifts in institutional culture and the shifts in feelings of people who work here and we respond and react to that and do something about it rather than ignore it.

"No matter how well things are run you always have to be attuned to potential issues and be ready to deal with them. That runs across the piece, whether the curriculum, people and relationships or behaviour. It's like sailing a boat. You have to be sensitive to changes in the wind and take account of that, otherwise you will suddenly find you are becalmed or in completely the wrong place."

A collective process

School leaders constantly have to make micro-choices and it is important to be able to judge what your priorities are, says Alison Peacock, Headteacher of The Wroxham primary school in Potters Bar, Hertfordshire. For her the priorities are always about the people in her school – a useful tip for first-time heads who are new to the job.

"I think you learn pretty quickly as a head. You are thrown in pretty much at the deep end. When you are newly appointed there are obviously things you have never done before. If you are reflective then you will think, 'How did that go? Could it have gone better? Could I have handled this differently?' Judgement is about being able to weigh up everything you understand about a situation and that comes from actively listening to people. You need to be an active listener, you need to be reflective and you need to talk to people. It's not about thinking, 'I'm going to sit on my own and make a decision and everyone is just going to have to abide by it'.

"Very often it's a collective process with people asking, 'Is this the right way to go?' If you are building a team around you who are future leaders they are going to feel empowered enough to say, 'Yes, but last time we did this, this happened'. It's important to have that genuine debate because if you surround yourself with people who are just going to agree with you then there is no point asking them. It's important to have that genuine sense of challenge and dialogue that is centred on a clear vision of what the school is about.

"It's about saying collectively, what do we all think about this and how can we find a way through it? There are always going to be difficult things that hit you for the first time that you haven't had before. Part of the attraction of the job is that things constantly occur for the first time."

According to Bernard Trafford, Headmaster of the Royal Grammar School in Newcastle, the best school leaders "have the ability to pull all the pieces together, see the gaps and take action to bridge or plug them". They are able "to make the organisation consistent and coherent and also to make and justify tough decisions".

"It's a thing that's both born and learned, because you can't replace experience. If you are going to be a good head you are born with a fair sense of judgement. But the other thing you need to do is to take advice; don't rush in without consulting other people first. Sometimes you have to carry people with you and that's all the more reason for getting them round the table. If you are doing something that requires some tricky decisions you don't have to do it on your own. And frankly you sleep better if you are not left on your own wondering if you've done the right thing."

Involving the team

Good judgement is usually a combination of intuition and experience. It is important for a school leader to have good instincts and be prepared to act on them. Even so, a wise leader should never be autocratic and should involve other team members when taking important decisions, says Teresa Tunnadine, Headteacher of The Compton School in North London.

"As in all organisations you are making hundreds of judgements all the time, from the colour of paint on the wall to decisions about how you are going to spend a budget of £80 million. There are decisions from micro to macro. The important thing for me is to use a balance of experience of what's gone before, and what's worked well and what hasn't, with a kind of gut feeling, or intuition. Part of that gut feeling comes from experience anyway. I will increasingly rely on instinct but I guess that's grounded in experience because I've been a senior leader for a very long time. I have experienced lots of different scenarios and have learned from those experiences.

"I also have three senior colleagues who I will talk to all the time. So if there are decisions that are worrying me they will be worrying us all. We will canvas opinion and go through it and often sleep on it and we will not be afraid to change tack. I am also quite able to be decisive but I guess that's because I've done the job for a while and have learned the things that have and haven't worked. I don't get it right all the time but if I don't I'm quite happy to put my hand up and say, 'That was the wrong call'. I will do that in front of the staff as a whole as well as individuals.

"Making the right judgements about the staff we appoint is absolutely critical and I will surround myself with people so that we make those decisions collectively. That's really helpful. It's never about me taking autocratic decisions. Occasionally we will get to the point where a decision has got to be made and there's a 50-50 split within the team and I have to come down and say 'This is the thing we are going to do', but it really doesn't happen very often. Decisions usually come out of a lot of thought and discussion involving a number of people and then we reach a consensus.

"The other important thing is choosing the battles to fight and the battles not to fight and that goes back to moral purpose. We were involved in a court case where there was a woman who had a mental illness, a member of staff who wasn't with us for very long. We could have paid her off to go away but she was making pretty outrageous accusations against another member of staff and I thought, 'Actually this isn't about the money, it's about clearing the name of a person who was being slandered. It was a judgement call. I could have taken the easy way out but decided not to and it ended up in a tribunal which we won. I felt we were vindicated even though it was quite painful on the way. There have been a number of very difficult cases like that where your judgement is not to take the easy way out and I won't take the easy way out if I think there's a moral issue at stake."

Patricia Scott, Headteacher of St Luke's High School in Barrhead, East Renfrewshire, also believes that making important judgements is something that should be shared. Leaders should take their time to consider all the angles and reflect on them before coming to a conclusion.

"I think the ability to make judgements gets better with experience. It's something headteachers have to do day in, day out: making judgement calls, knowing when to push, when to support or when to take one decision rather than another. I think that making wise judgements is absolutely critical and taking the time to do it is really important, so it's not just a knee-jerk reaction. You have to think it through. It is something that has to be shared with everyone in the team," she says.

"Many judgements are strategic and you do need to take time to discuss them and share them with others. It might be a judgement you need to make about the next direction for the school improvement plan. It's an opportunity to reflect on what you are planning, to bounce ideas off the senior leadership team, or an individual group of youngsters, parents or staff. There are judgements being made at all levels all the time and it's important to get them right. A lot of judgements are instinctive, because you've been there before so many times. And some of them are strategic judgements that require a lot of background and consideration before a judgement is taken."

Wisdom through experience

Richard Harman, Headmaster of Uppingham School in Rutland, believes that leading a successful school requires considerable wisdom, something that needs to be acquired. A great headteacher, he says, "knows when to act quickly and when to reflect, when to 'nudge' and when to intervene, who to talk to and how to listen: something that only comes with experience".

"As a head you have to play a lot of roles. You could be cast as chief executive, priest, counsellor or educational visionary. One of them is the wise owl – a Gandalf, or a Dumbledore figure," he says.

This wise owl is frequently to be found, metaphorically-speaking, sitting on his shoulder.

"It's something that comes with time and experience to some extent. I think occasionally I have made the mistake of thinking that because I'm nudging people, they are getting the message. You have got to know when people you nudge take it seriously and when they don't. It's also about being a good judge of people because some people will not respond to a direct response, in words of one syllable, whereas they will respond to a 'Don't you think it would be a nice idea if...?' sort of approach. There are others who do need you to be very direct."

Mike Kent, former Headteacher of Comber Grove Primary School in Camberwell, South London, says it is important to be able "to recognise, almost intuitively, which aspects of a school aren't working well". Leaders also need to "be sensitive, sympathetic and understanding towards people" and "to listen to everybody's view, but then be decisive in action".

This sense of intuitive wisdom works best when a leader knows his or her school well, he says.

> "It becomes much easier if you know your school, if you visit your classrooms and are out and about. You can get a feel for whether maybe literacy isn't quite as good as it should be in Year 3 or you're not doing as much in the infant playground as you should to make sure children have games at lunchtime to stop them running around fighting each other. It's a case of having a feel of what's going well or what's not. You talk to staff all the time. There will be ripples that you pick up on. Someone will be worried about a particular thing or a curriculum leader may say there are difficulties in getting the results I need from Year 5. You have got to take on all these things. You have to prioritise and decide what's important."

Moral leadership

Madeleine Vigar, Principal of the Castle Partnership Academy Trust in Haverhill, Suffolk, says that the experience she gained "treading the boards" as a classroom teacher for 20 years was crucial in preparing her for the tough decisions she has had to make as a headteacher.

> "Judgement is absolutely crucial in good leadership. At the end of the day you are the key leader in school and you have to make decisions about some difficult things because issues in schools are quite often not black and white. You don't always know if you're right or wrong to be honest, but you're the one given the task of making judgements. To inform your judgement you use past experiences and you use intuition about the way people are. It's a combination.
>
> "School leadership is, without doubt about moral leadership. It's very different to the type of leadership I experienced when I worked in industry for a year. What we are doing in school every day is making decisions and judgements all day long about the direction a child can go in, or what direction a colleague can go in. In industry you have to make big decisions about big money deals, but it's not something you do all the time. You're performing and modelling all the time in the school as a headteacher."

One of the most critical aspects of a headteacher's role is being able 'to see both the wood and the trees', says Vigar. She first heard the phrase in a leadership context from Professor Dame Pat Collarbone, the former Head of the London Leadership Centre at London University's Institute of Education, who led the development of the National Professional Qualification for Headship (NPQH) in 1999.

> "I was in one of the first cohorts to get the NPQH and it was something Dame Pat said in a speech when she was handing out the certificates. She stood up and said, 'Leadership is the ability to see both the wood and the trees'. We use that phrase here at Castle Manor every single day when we have our leadership meetings. As a leadership team we often ask ourselves 'What is the difference between the wood and the trees?' – now known as wood items and trees items in our daily briefing book. In schools, there are trees-items that happen all the time, little things like, 'Do I open the door for this child?', or 'That loo seat is broken in the girls' loos and it needs mending'. Things like that are constant in

schools – they lie underneath the bigger wood issues, such as: 'We treat each other with respect here'.

"When I started at Castle Manor nine years ago I introduced a rule where when I walk into a classroom the children stand up. You could see it as a trees-issue, but it's not about that at all. It was a key part of modelling respect and good behaviour in a school where behaviour had deteriorated. If I took you into one of our classrooms now you would see a huge difference compared to what was the worst school in Suffolk.

"Recently I set the staff a task to think back to that time and why we did that. It's about sharing values, so sometimes underpinning the trees-objects are bigger wood-issues. We try to use it in the leadership team as an exercise, asking ourselves, 'Can we see the difference between the trees and wood?' Underpinning all this is moral purpose and values, which is very important in school leaders."

That sense of moral underpinning can be critical when leaders have to make finely balanced judgements about the future direction of their school, says Maggie Farrar, former Executive Director of the National College for School Leadership.

"This really comes to the fore when there's a fine balance between decisions. Often when it is a fine balance and a head has to make a decision which isn't going to be popular with everybody, that's when they go back to their core principles, their moral purpose, their vision, and say "I've made this call for these reasons," and people can accept it."

Competing priorities

Often, those decisions require leaders to make difficult choices between competing priorities, says Andrew Fleck, Headmaster of Sedbergh School, an independent boarding establishment in Cumbria.

"There are limited resources in terms of time, money and skills and it is essential to deploy these efficiently and with clear priority. Prioritisation is painful because it disappoints people but it is essential in order to achieve outcomes."

The ability to make those painful choices and to implement necessary changes is something that improves with experience, says Fleck. As an example, he cites his own experience as a first-time headteacher at Ashville College, Harrogate, compared with his current headship at Sedbergh: "I survived my first year at Ashville. At Sedbergh we achieved a lot. The first year at Ashville, I appointed a secretary and sacked the bursar and that was it. The first year at Sedbergh, I appointed a new management team; introduced a new school week; a new curriculum for Years 7 to 9; all the staff are now involved in weekend arrangements; I appointed four new housemasters and housemistresses; built a new health centre and a new music centre; created a new marketing structure and changed the Old Sedberghians' Club and its relationship with the school. The contrast could not be more marked."

Staff appointments

Some of the most important judgements headteachers have to make involve staff appointments and ensuring the right people are in the right jobs, says Russell Hinton, Headteacher of The Brier School, a special school for children with moderate learning difficulties in Kingswinford, Dudley, in the West Midlands.

"You have to look at the team you've got and within that team there are always going to be weak links and people with particular strengths and it's important how you deal with those. As a manager you have to know your staff first and you have to have the evidence on why they are good. Rather than say, 'Why is someone bad?' it's better to ask, 'Why is somebody better than that person?' 'How are they able to do the job better?'

"You start from that point of strength rather than a point of weakness. So you ask, 'What makes a good teacher in this particular school, The Brier? How do they adapt to having four-year-olds, a Foundation Stage and four Key Stages, with 16-year-olds moving onto further education?' Could they teach in different parts of the school? Some couldn't and some could. That's how you use your staff. Some would be better and feel more confident in a particular area than others. It's a case of looking at what they can do in the establishment."

Key qualities

To be successful, school leaders need to be able to draw upon a number of key qualities and to find the right balance between them. They need vision, courage and a passionate belief in helping children to achieve well and develop into well-rounded individuals. Many of the key decisions they have to make, both big and small, wood-issues and trees-issues, require an intuitive understanding of the people in their school community. Emotional intelligence, including the skills of:

- empathy
- understanding
- a willingness to listen to competing views

is especially important. What sets judgement apart as a key leadership quality is that it is about finding the right balance. It is not just about taking the right decisions to take a school forward; it is about involving the whole school community in shaping the future and taking them forward together.

6
Resilience

Successful school leaders are optimistic and resilient. They are energetic and positive and remain calm in a crisis.

The business of headship is full-on and at times gruelling. This is particularly so in inner-city schools which are under-performing and undergoing much-needed change. For many headteachers resilience – the ability to cope with setbacks, disappointments or the inevitable frustrations of leadership – is absolutely vital. This can come with experience but is also part of the personality and aptitude of successful headteachers.

"Heads need to be positive and optimistic and not be overwhelmed when things don't go according to plan or when the government comes up with some new and seemingly impossible target or initiative. Children and staff need someone who can help them see that the future is bright and that anything is possible," says Kenny Frederick, Principal of George Green's School in Tower Hamlets, East London.

Outwardly, this requires the headteacher in a school to be a beacon of positivity, radiating hopefulness, good humour, calm reassurance and resolution. Inwardly, she or he needs to be able to draw on a well of personal qualities, coping strategies and beliefs. The well may be fed by the headteacher's innate sense of optimism and high energy levels but also needs to be topped up in many other ways. Headteachers need to be able to draw strength from their personal beliefs and values, from their own experience as teachers and leaders and rely on support from colleagues, friends and family. They also need to find space within their busy lives to look after themselves; to pursue outside interests and to stay fit and healthy.

Developing resilience

Catherine Paine, Executive Headteacher of Mount Street Academy and Saxilby Church of England Primary School in Lincolnshire, says it is important to have "the ability to look like everything is under control, even when it isn't, and inspire confidence in others".

> "It is all about resilience. It's also about really knowing yourself and having personal strategies so you are able to steady yourself in stormy waters. There's just no scope for a headteacher to have a bad hair day. You are not forgiven for it and nobody is interested in hearing what your burdens are. So it's about being able to go into each exchange, each meeting, each scenario, each engagement with a teacher or in a lesson, as if that's the only thing that you're doing that day.
>
> "Everybody requires of you and deserves your best and therefore what's gone on in the last half-hour or three hours, or that week, is of no concern to the children and really no concern of the teachers. I feel that some of the headteachers I meet who lack resilience are just not robust enough to be able to cope with the torrent of things that come their way during the course of the day."

Developing resilience is one of the most important requirements for a school leader who wishes to be successful and maintain their commitment and motivation over a long career. Successful headteachers tend to develop their own regimes to help them relax, keep their energy levels high, refresh themselves and achieve a sense of perspective. Paine, who became one of the youngest headteachers in Britain in 1998, at the age of 28, relies on a mixture of meditation and long-distance running to sustain her.

"I get up at 5am and I meditate for an hour. For me, that's something that works. I also run long distances. On the surface they are completely non-productive things to do and yet to me they are vital to retaining equanimity of mind. That's what you have to strive for, because you can guarantee that during the course of a day in a challenging school something will be heading your way to knock you off course. And it's not that you don't feel the impact when it does, but you don't let it turn the vessel over. You have to maintain a steady course.

"Some of that is about growing resilience which is what I always aim to do in a day. It's always an aspiration, if not a reality, not to leave that place of peace and tranquillity that I experienced early in the morning. If I can keep that with me during the course of the day, where I know there's a place in which I am untouchable – a place of peace and serenity and magnanimity and compassion – it actually does change the way you think. It builds you time in, you are less reactive, your touch-paper is not so easily lit. You are able to take the bigger picture into consideration rather than shooting from the hip, or crumbling under pressure.

"It wouldn't work for everybody but that's the kind of thing I mean when I say it's about you looking like everything is under control. First of all you have to find an experience where authentically you can say, 'There is a place within me where everything is under control'. Someone once said to me in my first year of headship, 'A bad day is only a bad day if you'll remember it in ten years' time'. I have got a few of them, but not that many. It's trying to keep the bigger picture in mind all the time. You might feel, 'I'm having a horrendous day, but really it's just bread and butter stuff that I'm not going to remember even next week.'"

Belief

Paine also speaks of the importance of "faith, or something close to it, leading to deeply held values about human flourishing" in guiding leaders and shaping their decisions.

"You have to believe in something for yourself and have some kind of ongoing journey. Whether that's the Christian path, the Buddhist path or the humanist path doesn't really matter as long as you believe in something. What meditation does for me is it's a great leveller and you are reminded that there is a lot more in common we have with our fellow man than separates us. It helps not to view anyone as hostile, or as an adversary. It helps one to view somebody that might look like they are intent on causing you or your system harm more sympathetically. It makes you unafraid of dealing with people who are marginalised in society. We all have emotions. We all want to be happy and want to avoid suffering.

"There is so much that connects us to other people but I think sometimes heads have a temptation to become paranoid. It can seem an ever-present threat. You can be pretty sure that someone, somewhere, is saying something you would rather not hear. It's important to find ways of viewing the world with generosity. How someone does that doesn't really matter. John West-Burnham uses that phrase, 'reservoirs of hope', where he talks about becoming personally authentic as well as personally effective. Being authentic means you have got to create and nurture some sort of reservoir of hope which empowers you to take on new challenges and approach the future with confidence. It gives you a sense of optimism and orientates your heart."

Professor West-Burnham, who first used the phrase in 2002, returns to the theme in his recent book *Rethinking Educational Leadership* (Continuum, 2009), in which he argues that effective leaders need strategies to ensure that their reservoirs are regularly filled. Paine agrees that there is an ever-present danger that the well will run dry and that school leaders who start out as idealists risk losing their sense of hope or their passion for the job.

"It's why organisations become hopeless – when their leaders become hopeless. Personally I am responsible for keeping my reservoir topped up and also wherever possible I do everything I can to top up my staff's reservoirs. It's also important to have a work-life balance policy. We have a policy of one pyjama day per term where somebody can book a day off for their mother's 80th birthday, for their child's birthday, or to go Christmas shopping.

"It's about relaxation and restoration, an opportunity to top up their reservoirs because it is a full-on job. I will never forget not being able to spend my son's first birthday with him. You work full time but you really don't want not to see your child on his first birthday. I often get emails from staff saying thank you for introducing pyjama days, I will never forget that occasion. People do give more willingly because they see that you recognise that they are human beings as well as members of staff."

Taking the long view

Paine emphasises the importance of taking the long view as a school leader, both professionally and personally, and "being able to say, amidst complexity and confusion, 'I know where I'm going'". It helps, she says, to have tenacity: "a dogged determination to never, never give up."

"There are definite days and experiences where the temptation to say 'I can't do this anymore' or 'I'm going to have a rethink' is quite an alluring temptation. Particularly for me becoming a head so young, with the pension age continuing to go up I could be a head for 40 years. It's a case of viewing yourself as a marathon runner, not as a sprinter. It's having that sense of 'I'm holding on for a long journey'. Sometimes not wanting everything to be resolved by tomorrow is a realistic view to have; you are holding out for the prize at the end. When I run long distance I go through all the human emotions. It becomes like a metaphor for life really. You feel elation and despair all within the space of two hours.

"Now I have a bit of experience under my belt I can look round and see some of the dark days I've been in and can see how eventually they have been resolved for the good. I can look back now and say, well that door closed but this door opened. It gives you a bit more perspective on things. The long view is very important because sometimes things do become very complex and confusing and it becomes very tempting to give in because it is just too hard.

"I suppose it's about beginning every single new day with that sense of renewed confidence and belief in yourself and those around you. It's about believing in what children deserve to have during these precious years of their lives and then communicating that to all the people around you and then being able to say, 'Do you know I don't know how I came through that time but it all worked out for the good'."

Spiritual and emotional resilience

Richard Harman, Headmaster of Uppingham School in Rutland, one of England's great public boarding schools, is another who believes in the importance of building resilience ("a much under-rated quality" in leaders, he says). He too is a keen advocate of keeping fit in order to cope with the physical and mental pressures of the job. But he also stresses the importance of developing spiritual and emotional resilience.

"I need to keep myself fit because there's a danger you could spend your whole time in this job sitting down or standing up and making speeches. I was diagnosed with type-2 diabetes about four years ago and I have to exercise, otherwise I will get ill. It's been very good for me because it's forced me to include exercise in my week which I didn't do before. On a very basic level the physical matters. But it's also about emotional intelligence, self-awareness and resilience. It's about taking time to reflect, or pray, in order to do what is a very busy job and being ready to make decisions one after the other when you need to.

"There are some times when all the news seems to be challenging and one problem comes on top of another and you have to deal with all of them. Resilience is more than just the ability to bounce back regardless, like one of those figures on a spring.

"The thing is that everyone in the community takes their cue from you. If you are looking tired and fed up they will all say there's something wrong. They will all feel tired and fed up too. You can't be Panglossian about everything but to keep some optimism, a reservoir of hope that people can tap into, is very important. When things look bleak or dark and everyone else is flapping you need to be able to say well, you may not see it now but there will be a solution. That ability to bounce back and see the positives is really important."

Llyn Codling, Executive Headteacher of Portswood and St Mary's Church of England Primary Schools in Southampton, believes in the value of meditation as a means of controlling the mind: "No one else is going to do that for you and if you're not careful you can go out of control," she says.

"I'm a yoga teacher in my spare time. I teach the children as well as adults that we are responsible for our own minds. You can either go into negative mind and downward spiral, you can go into positive mind which is great, but quite dangerous, or sometimes you need to go into that neutral space and look at things very neutrally. It helps when you have to take difficult decisions. For example – and I'm not going into any details – but there are two bits of me. There is the professional headteacher that will talk to you very neutrally, and then there's the human bit that's standing like the chattering monkey on the sidelines going 'oh my goodness'. I have to get rid of that chattering monkey and I have to go into the professional neutral headteacher bit of me to be able to deal with something appropriately. That's what I mean by controlling your own mind."

Radiating positivity

Ani Magill, Headteacher of St John the Baptist School in Woking, Surrey, stresses the importance of radiating positivity as a school leader.

"I do think that the leaders at all levels set the emotional climate, and we all know what it's like to meet somebody and to be with somebody for ten minutes who drains all the life out of you. At SJB we say that as leaders we've got to get out there and be really positive with people. So we have loads of rules here about 'no negative messages', ever: not in public, not for the children, and never, ever anything negative in assemblies.

"We would never, in a staff briefing or a staff meeting, say 'People haven't done this', or 'You must do that', or 'This isn't good enough'. That would never happen. All the public venues, all the public meetings are used to thank people and to praise people. So we praise in public and bollock in private. We used to say 'Never remove a child's fig leaf in public' and it's the same for a member of staff."

Maintaining that public positivity in the face of the daily challenges of school leadership can be demanding. It helps, says Magill, to have a good sense of humour (during this interview she was wearing a pink onesie for the day to raise money for charity) and she and her leadership team set the climate by encouraging the children and staff to 'have a laugh'. School leaders also need to make time to look after themselves, and their staff too.

"If you work in an environment where people are very positive it does make you feel more positive yourself. But I do think that as headteachers, if we don't look after ourselves, we can't look after anyone else. Personally, I'm very physically fit. I do a lot of sport, I eat really well, I sleep a lot, I really look after myself. And we have a lot of things that we do in school where we try to make sure that we really cherish the staff and enable them to look after themselves, so that they're fresh and positive for the children.

"We do lots of little things. We get people's dry cleaning done and their cars MOT'd. I just went into the staff room and saw bars of chocolate in people's pigeon holes. That was because some staff helped with a revision evening and the person who leads that group put a bar of chocolate in all their pigeon holes just to say thank you. There are a hundred little things like that that happen all day every day. It is about the leaders looking after themselves and reminding themselves and reminding everybody else what a privilege it is to have the job that we've got."

Alison Peacock, Headteacher of The Wroxham primary school in Potters Bar, Hertfordshire, describes resilience as "a key quality". It is about learning to deal with adversity and the pressures of the job while outwardly maintaining a sense of calmness, consistency and positivity, she says.

"There have been times when I have cried in school but it's not usually been to do with the job. There was a time when my mother was very ill. It's fine for you to be human and for people to come up and sometimes put their arm around you and say, 'Are you all right today?' We don't have to pretend to be superhuman. But I think when things get difficult, if there is a crisis, I would always remain calm. It almost feels like the more challenging a situation is the more calm I become. People need reassurance from the leader and in a situation where something is difficult they need to feel there is a consistency, that you are going to listen and take things seriously and that you are going to act on what you say you are going to do. People need to see you as someone who can be trusted and believe that you will follow things through and won't shy away from what needs to be done.

"You do need to have a lot of energy as a school leader and positivity too. People respond so well when you can highlight success; if you can create that feeling that anything is possible then people, whether it is adults or children, want to work in that environment. They like to feel acknowledged and celebrated for what they are doing. They also like to think that the next step is within their reach and that they will be helped."

Steely determination

Creating that sense of optimism is essential if a school is going to be successful, says Roger Pope, Principal of Kingsbridge Community College in Devon. But you also need to have a steely determination if you want to build a culture of high expectations.

"There are lots of occasions where there is an easy and a hard way to go about things. The teacher who isn't delivering what he should be doing, the teacher who is late, the teacher who talks to kids in a way you don't want them to do; or the kids who are persistently late, or under-achieving. There is always a temptation to let them get away with it. You need resilience and courage in terms of always being ready to take people on, if you think that that's the right thing to do. If I was to draw a graph of it, the more you build that culture of high expectations, the less you have to do that."

He also stresses the importance of the role played by a headteacher and the need to be positive and remain strong.

> "You can never underestimate the amount of notice that people take of what you say. There are many occasions where people will say to me, 'Remember when you said to me...' and it will have been four, five or six years ago and about something profoundly important to them. You forget that you have hundreds of interactions a day or a week as a headteacher. But for somebody on the staff that might have been the only time you've spoken to them in a fortnight and it sticks in their mind. So I do think you need to be enormously resilient because you cannot afford to show any weakness, any tiredness, or any depression. You have to have a cheerful smiley face on you all the time. Given the amount of interactions you have during the course of a day that mask can slip and if it does you know you've done wrong and you shouldn't have let it happen."

Work-life balance

Coping with the many pressures of headship can be challenging and successful school leaders frequently speak about the importance of being able to rely on colleagues, personal friendships and family for support. Roger Pope is one of these. He also believes in keeping a sensible balance between work and private life.

"I have a very strong and close leadership team and sometimes if I do something I will go into them and say 'I've just said this to X and I don't think I should have done. What do you think?' That's one of my coping strategies. I have also got a very happy and stable family background that is my source of strength. Over the years I have delegated a lot of my tasks to other people. I am quite careful in terms of my work-life balance because I know that I can't afford to come in and be teary or tired. So I try and stay pretty centred."

Unlike some very successful leaders who often work punishingly long hours, Pope believes this is unsustainable over a long career and in many cases can be a sign of ineffectiveness.

"I don't do that. I get in at 7.45am every morning and am usually here till about 6pm. My view is that if you are working during that ten hour day and you are there 100 per cent all the time, you should be able to get everything done. If not, what are you doing?"

Richard Harman is another leader who emphasises the value of having strong support from close colleagues and family.

"You wouldn't get through all the challenges without good people around you, people like your deputy and PA. They are the unsung heroes. You absolutely have to have that support network around you. If one part of that support network breaks down or is in trouble, then *you* might be in trouble. If you don't have that you are not going to be able to perform or cope. You can't control all of what happens to you, but you have to have a healthy base," he says.

School leaders need to make time to ensure they have adequate support networks in place and that they in turn are well supported. Failure to do so can have disastrous consequences, both personal and professional.

"It's a big danger because it's a very natural response to all the pressures you face to find an area of life where you can withdraw into yourself," says Harman. "We all want to feel safe and of course all relationships involve challenge. It happens to me sometimes. You've had a terrible day, you go home and all you want to do is to 'veg out' or have a bit of time to yourself. But you have to respond to the demands of your child, or your spouse, your partner. And sometimes they will challenge you about what you're doing as well. You have to be able to see that as support rather than as a threat."

Family and personal friends can provide crucial support, especially if a leader is new in a post and trying to introduce significant changes in practice, says Lynn Slinger, Headteacher of Forest Way Special School in Coalville, Leicestershire.

"Being a head can be the best job in the world but it can also be the worst and the loneliest job in the world too. When I came to this school I had the governors on my side but I knew that most of the staff thought what I was doing was unlike anything they had ever seen. It was a real culture shock. You need resilience, when everyone in the school is against you, to carry on until you reach your aim at the end. That takes a lot of hard steeliness from within.

"A lot of my resilience comes from friends and family outside school. When you are in a job that's very tough you need to have something in your life to balance it. I can find the resilience to carry on against all odds at work as long as at home I've got security and support. I've got a very supportive marriage, a small but very supportive family and some very good friends. They give me the emotional support I need away from school and that really helps me."

Staying positive

Slinger also speaks of the importance of developing a positive culture in a school.

"It's the pot half-empty, pot half-full scenario. Even if things are bad as a leader and a manager you have to be positive and you have to find solutions rather than problems all the time. And you've got to transfer that to staff to get a positive working ethos. It's about staff learning to bring solutions themselves. I might not choose the solution or it might be one of three possible scenarios. What matters is having a positive way forward through very difficult times, rather than always being negative. I think that has to come from the top but the aim must be eventually to get a school where the solutions come from the bottom-up as well as top-down. Once you've got that all the way through an organisation you know it's really working well."

Madeleine Vigar, Principal of The Castle Partnership Academy Trust in Haverhill, Suffolk, speaks about the importance of being able to radiate optimism and positivity as a school leader.

"The mantra has to be at all times that you're optimistic and the leadership team here know that. They can be pessimistic when they're in here [the office] if they want to, but out there you have to be swan-like and optimistic at all times. And it's not just me, it's the whole leadership team and it should be teachers as well. That takes a personal toll on you. You get absolutely exhausted by the end of the day. But that's what you have got to do in certain schools. I have worked in five or six schools and all of them have had children who can be more challenging. But in all of those schools that is the strategy that works."

A sense of humour

Humour can help a school leader stay positive and keep them going whenever they have to deal with stressful situations. For this reason it is important to choose the right people to work with, says Vigar.

"You should always be able to laugh at yourself and to laugh with others. Humour is absolutely key when it comes to building relationships with youngsters and with the leadership team."

By way of example, she describes a leadership meeting held on the morning of a geography Ofsted inspection, shortly after the police had called to complain about the school not using the 'No Parking' bollards they had provided.

"That started quite an interesting conversation about bollards as you can imagine. It helped to have that bit of silliness to come out at the end of the meeting because actually all of us are a bit childlike really. None of us should take ourselves that seriously."

Devon Hanson, Principal of Evelyn Grace Academy in Brixton, also thinks that humour is important to lighten up a long meeting. It is part of the glue that holds teams together.

"I like to make a joke about myself at times in staff briefings so that staff can have a laugh. It's good for them to laugh even if it's at my expense because I still have the confidence a few minutes later to say, 'OK that's done, we have to talk the serious talk now'. One of the good things about my senior leadership team is we often have three-hour meetings but you can guarantee there will be laughter within that. I will make sure they're laughing and there is humour even when we are discussing serious things."

Paul Smith, Principal of Parbold Douglas Church of England Academy, a rural primary school in Lancashire, says a sense of humour helps a leader to keep their own sanity as well as that of their team.

> "I find it helps to keep a sense of perspective that can be easily lost when we find ourselves up to our ears in the trenches. Humour helps to develop team spirit and get people on side with you even if at times it is a delirious or gallows humour. We have to remember that as headteacher we are responsible for setting the mood and the ethos for the school so the best headteachers can turn some of the most dire circumstances into positives or points for future development. It's amazing how a bit of blue sky thinking – and talking – can turn the gloomiest day around."

Having a good sense of humour is often cited as a key leadership attribute. So too is the ability to let go at the end of a long day. The business of school leadership, especially for those who are most successful, tends to be all-consuming. Different leaders employ different strategies or rely on their outside activities to relax. For Lynn Slinger, relaxation comes in the form of exotic foreign holidays, something she did not feel the need for until she became a head.

"That has helped my resilience. I just go into a different state and that's what gives me the resilience to come back to do the job full-on seven days a week. I can do that as long as I have these little oases of time that give me total time out. Other people don't do it in that way, but that's been my real life-saver really," she says.

Never-ending demands

Russell Hinton, who took up his present post as Headteacher of The Brier special school in Kingswinford, Dudley, in 2005, recognises that the enormously demanding physical and emotional nature of the job "does eat into your psyche".

"I can't speak for others but I sleep and dream about my school. In the summer holidays if I'm not abroad I will be in school. I might be on the beach and my wife will turn to me and say, 'You're thinking about the school again aren't you?' You can't stop. It does consume you," he says.

His recommendation to other heads is "to accept that you will never finish the day with everything done. You are not indispensible".

"That was the best bit of advice I've ever had and it came from my assistant director in Dudley. As a new head I went to some induction meetings. It was a shock to come to Dudley because I found myself getting upwards of 60 emails a day, all of them saying they were urgent, which I didn't have in my previous borough. I also had to deal with all the things that were going on in the school. I just said, what is this email culture about, why can't people just pick up the phone anymore? And she said, 'Just remember Russell, you will never lock that door at the end of the day and think you've finished, because you never do finish.' As long as I know I've done my best for that day I can come back to it tomorrow."

The risk of burnout

For many heads, even some of the best, the risk of mental and physical burnout is very real, partly because of their great dedication and commitment. They need to keep a sense of perspective and continue to believe in what they are doing. They also need to recognise that there will be setbacks and that they cannot hope to control everything.

> "The reality is that no matter what your best efforts are things can still come out not how you want them to and you've got to be able to bounce back from these situations and then come at them another way," says Patricia Scott, Headteacher of St Luke's High School in Barrhead, East Renfrewshire, Scotland.
>
> "That is life. The whole ebb and flow of school life requires you to deal with so many people, so many different situations, that you have to be ready when things don't go just as planned. You need to be ready to say, 'OK, let's come back at this in another way', or know when to leave things alone. I think that is really, really important, because we're dealing with situations that we have different levels of control over. That forces you to be resilient.
>
> "You have to stay strong. That's when the whole idea of the team comes into play. In many situations you're coming back to the drawing board, you're looking at, 'Where do we go to now?' 'Who needs to get involved in this decision, who do we need to consult with, who do we need support from?' It's important to be able to remember that moving forward is not down to any one person. You can't do it on your own, there has to be buy-in from everyone."

If the senior leadership team and other members of staff can play a vital supporting role when the going gets tough it often falls on the headteacher to motivate and inspire confidence in others. Dame Joan McVittie, Headteacher of Woodside High School in North London, learned a great deal about resilience from her former boss Sir Michael Wilshaw.

"Mike Wilshaw always had a phrase when you were a bit down. He'd talk to you and then he'd say to you, 'Now get back in there and fight the good fight'. That to me just sums it all up. It is about picking yourself up. Very often I tell the children in the school the story about Robert the Bruce and the spider. That's one that I relate to. I do think you need a huge amount of resilience. You've got to have the ability to keep coming back and focusing on your moral purpose. That's what gives you the resilience really to do all the difficult things."

Optimism and self-belief

Resilience is especially important in the often demanding context of inner-city schools. Devon Hanson, who has spent his entire career working in inner-London schools, believes it is an essential attribute for anyone who wants a successful career in teaching.

"Whenever I interview for any new member of staff there is that one word, 'resilience' that I want to hear from them. If I don't hear that word, or one which means the same thing, then I'm dubious. You need it as a headteacher but you also need it as a teacher in the type of schools that I've worked in. People say to me, 'You've spent your whole career in tough challenging schools'. I don't find them tough. They are challenging, it takes a lot of hard work, but I could look worse, even though I say it myself!"

Hanson, who in 2012 started his second headship at one of London's most high profile academies, can afford to make a joke of it. But the challenges of running a busy inner-city comprehensive can be daunting. Leaders who do take up the challenge need plenty of optimism and self-belief.

One of the most striking things about the school leaders interviewed for this book is their obvious passion for headship and the feeling that they can make a real difference. Teresa Tunnadine, Headteacher of The Compton School in North London, is typical of these. She is adamant that all the pressure and all the shocks that can come with the job are all worthwhile.

"It's the best job for me. I've loved this much more than I have coming all the way up through the ranks although for the first two or three years as a head I thought, 'What on earth have I done? This is so hard!' What for me works is keeping my energy levels up. I have naturally got a lot of energy and I think that helps. I'm fortunate that I don't often go down with colds and coughs and that kind of thing and that helps. It's important to put on a mask of calm and that becomes you, you grow into it.

"I am now able not just to show it on the outside but increasingly feel it on the inside. It's partly because I'm surrounded by brilliant people who are a joy to work with and partly because I've been a head for 13 years so most things have happened before. Sometimes things come along from out of left field that you can never really anticipate but I think once you've been through difficult events in the school's history you think 'Well, I've survived that so I can survive anything'. It's my job to steady the ship.

"One of my staff once said to me, 'You'd be standing upright in a force ten gale'. I wouldn't, but it's very nice that his perception of me is that I would be the rock that the school needs. That doesn't mean to say that my senior staff don't see me in a human way, they do. They see my faults and foibles and nervousness and I think that's important too.

"But you have to expect the unexpected. One of my previous chairs of governors said to me, 'Build in time for the unexpected and the difficult' and that's what I do. I try not to pack my diary. I try to give myself time, because that's part of the head's role, to deal with the unexpected and therefore to have the capacity to deal with it. It might be the death of a student, a court case or a whole department being out on maternity leave. Again it's back to moral purpose. I do it because the job is so valuable. The more you do it the more you are outwardly calm and the more energy you feel."

Charting a way through those storms and rough waters can be especially fulfilling, says Tunnadine.

"It is very satisfying if you can bring yourself and those around you through. There are always opportunities to be had, always things to be learned, even from the most difficult experiences. Even adversity is useful because it makes you reflect on what you're doing and think that maybe you want to try to do it even better. All of that learning is very useful. Something good will come out of whatever happens and that's proved to be the case for me, time and time again. You just have to remind yourself when you are going through the difficult times that you will come through the other side and that things will be better as a result of what you have done.

"On a small level I was told during my first year of headship, 'Keep your desk very tidy and people will think that you're very organised' and that's what I do. I have a very tidy, calm, tranquil office and I think it's very important to present that image of calm resilience."

Personality

Kenny Frederick, Principal of George Green's School in East London, believes that resilience is something school leaders learn through experience. But it is also part of their personality, she says.

"I don't know why I'm resilient. I am naturally optimistic. I do always believe that things are going to be better and they usually are. That's something in my make-up. I think being able to laugh at the ridiculous things that happen and to get a team to deal with knock-backs in the same way is important. Because one of the things you have to do as a head is to pick people up again when they are down. You have to give them confidence that things will get better, that what they are doing is the right thing and that we have got a plan. You have to do that for other people so you have to believe in yourself. Thankfully even in the darkest days I have always felt that things will get better," she says.

Running an inner-city school, especially one like George Green's, which serves a neighbourhood with one of the highest child poverty rates in Britain and has a policy of being fully inclusive, can be particularly challenging for everyone in the school. The headteacher needs to be particularly resilient and be seen as calm and capable, no matter how difficult a situation.

"If you are the pessimist and say, 'God, it's all hopeless, what's the point?' that's no good to anybody. You have got to always say as the leader, 'We need to keep moving forward. It may not always be as fast as we'd like but at least it's in the right direction'. You have to stay calm. There's no point in falling to pieces. I would say to staff who deal with children who disclose abuse, which is one of the things we have to deal with, there's no point in going, 'Oh my God' then breaking into tears and falling apart yourself, when there's a kid waiting for you to try and help them through it. They might have been dealing with that abuse for years so you falling apart is not going to do them any good."

Testing moment

A particularly testing moment in Frederick's career came in the autumn of 2008 when the school was given a notice to improve by the school inspection service Ofsted. For a leader who had been recognised in previous inspection reports as 'outstanding' and for running a school with many good and outstanding features is was a devastating blow.

"The results that year were a disaster so I had a feeling that it wasn't going to be easy. The experience itself was horrible. We had an HMI who was totally cold and unemotional. He told us at 11 o'clock that we were satisfactory and then at 12 o'clock he just came into my office and said it was a notice to improve. That was a terrible shock. I felt a bit like a headless chicken. I was in my office and everybody was off doing dinner duty. I didn't want to just go out and tell them and I just sat there trying to think what to do. It was a horrible feeling.

"I was ready to resign because I felt that it was my fault. But I had to think about my staff because for me to just walk out the door and disappear would have left them high and dry and the same would have been true of the kids. That wouldn't have done any good. So I came back the next day and decided to carry on."

One of the reasons for the school's poor showing that year – the proportion of pupils gaining five or more GCSE grades A*–C, including English and maths, fell to 29 per cent – was Frederick's oppositions to using GNVQs (vocational qualifications then equivalent to four good GCSEs) to boost George Green's position in the school league tables.

"We believed everybody should do a language and we'd just changed that the year that Ofsted came in. That obviously brought our results down. Sometimes your principles and values don't do you any favours."

The school responded by going even further down its chosen route, offering the International Baccalaureate in the sixth form and changing the school curriculum to introduce four different academic and vocational pathways. In 2012, 55 per cent of Year 11s achieved five good GCSEs with English and maths and the school now has a thriving IB diploma programme. In March, 2013, Ofsted re-inspected the school and judged it to be "good" in every respect and the quality of teaching "good and increasingly outstanding".

Frederick believes her determination to carry on and not to buckle under the pressure of one bad Ofsted sends an important message to other school leaders to stick to their values and principles. No leader, however good, can be outstanding all the time, she says.

"If you look at the different reports we have had, the first Ofsted we had said we were an improving school and that I was a marvel as an outstanding leader. The next one we were good with outstanding features. Then we went into a notice to improve and I was absolute rubbish and a failure. The goalposts keep changing all the time. You have to recognise for yourself what is good. I know what's good, what's bad and what should have been better but I'm also aware our kids come from all sorts of places and I think we give them a good deal. I think that things are much better now academically and I hope that improvement will continue.

"I hope that our school will always be open to all members of the community and it is our job to meet their needs. We will never be top of any league tables because I'm not prepared to keep those kids out who need a place in a good school like ours. Being a truly inclusive school involves lots of inconvenience, lots of additional work, lots of additional cost, but those kids have a right to go to school in their local community and we all benefit. We've got to hold our own and add value for all of those kids. That's what we're trying to do and I think we're doing it pretty effectively.

"There's a point where you keep to your vision, your values and principles and it is those things that get you out of bed in the morning. It got me out of bed when I got a notice to improve. I had to go back in and say to staff, 'You know, I could have just curled up and stayed there'. But if you really believe in something that's what gets you through the difficult times and you have got to hold on to that."

7
Persuasion

Successful school leaders are confident
communicators and story-tellers. They are
great persuaders and listeners who can get
their message across to any audience.

The best headteachers are natural communicators and have the ability to
reach out to, persuade and influence people in many different contexts.
They are adept at using assemblies and other school platforms to communicate core values and beliefs and create the right ethos. They are confident
public speakers, able to get their message across to pupils, staff, parents,
governors and the wider community. They are good at one-to-one and small
group meetings, but can also turn their hand to large set-piece occasions.
They also have excellent written skills, something which they use to great
effect in letters, emails, newsletters, prospectuses and other forms of written
communication.

They are frequently at their best when representing or defending their
schools. They are comfortable at dealing with the media and adept at using
it to their advantage – not just willing but eager to communicate and engage
with the outside world. As successful school leaders they often have a great
story to tell – and they do it well.

Smooth operators

But while it is important to have all-round communication skills to be an effective headteacher or principal, you do not have to be a paragon with a golden tongue. Indeed, there is an instinctive distrust of the kind of smooth operator sometimes seen and heard at education events and conferences. What matters is that you have credibility and believe in what you say, according to Andrew Hutchinson, Executive Principal of Parkside Federation Academies in Cambridge.

"You have to be able to communicate at all levels to be an effective head. The essential thing is to make sure that your communication maintains that sense of credibility. There are heads who are effective communicators, who can give an effective presentation at a national level, but the audience doubts their credibility. Being credible is having resonance with people who can see that what you're doing is actually grounded in practice. An important part of being a communicator is conveying that sense that you actually believe it; that you believe it and you live it. You've got to have integrity. That takes you a huge way. If people see that you have integrity then so much else becomes a lot easier. That's true at all levels," Hutchinson says.

Great story-tellers

Maggie Farrar, former Executive Director of the National College for School Leadership, puts it another way.

"We all know people with golden tongues. They are very skilful communicators and as a result you can sometimes feel manipulated. The best school leaders are great communicators but I would say more than that; they are great story-tellers. They tell great stories. A story-teller holds the narrative of the school – where it is, where it's been and where it's going and is able to influence and persuade with the power of individual examples that everybody understands. It's the power of the narrative.

"So I'm not talking about a great communicator who's got 20 PowerPoint slides but someone who brings the hopes, the vision and the passion of the school alive. I would also say that great communicators are very skilled in the power of conversation. They are great listeners and ask great questions. They ask more questions than give answers in my view."

Sir Tim Brighouse, the former Commissioner for London Schools, himself a notable communicator, likens the headteacher's role to that of the ancient Scandinavian chronicler of folklore, the *skald*, who told stories to warriors before a battle.

"The stories were always positive and reminded people of past great deeds, as well as impending future triumphs. I suppose in our culture Shakespeare's construction of Harry's speech before Agincourt is an equivalence. It's the same with heads. There is a touch of the 'skaldic' about all the successful ones," says Brighouse in his book, *How Successful Headteachers Survive and Thrive* (RM, 2007). They use assemblies, awards ceremonies, staff meetings and other occasions to reflect on and celebrate success and to praise individual and team effort.

"Being a skald probably takes up three or four hours each week... It should not be confused with talking which happens all the time – but it does embrace both speaking to large and small groups and telling stories."

Assemblies offer leaders the chance to build a narrative about their school, allowing them to focus on:

- values
- ethos
- expectations
- achievements.

Making assemblies challenging and interesting "can be one of the most time-effective things you do: they set the tone," says Nigel Richardson, the now retired former Headteacher of The Perse School in Cambridge. Heads should use assemblies to "find original and inventive ways of emphasising regularly the importance of being kind, courteous and grateful to *all* members of the school community, regardless of their role or status – and practise what you preach," he says.

Bernard Trafford, Headmaster of the Royal Grammar School in Newcastle, believes that assemblies and staff meetings are an important way of bringing people together in an age where schools are increasingly complex and busy places. They also allow heads to set out plans and explain their vision.

"Why do I preach to the staff at the start of the term? I'm sure they dread it; but if I don't, if the head doesn't stand up and say what we're here for and talk about the ethos, then no-one will. Communication is about communicating the vision and why you're trying to push it, but it's also about trying to get people – stakeholders – into change and development," he says.

Becoming an effective communicator

Very successful school leaders often take naturally to this story-telling role. They are able to create a narrative for their schools and carry people along with them, sometimes through sheer force of personality. Frequently they are seen as charismatic or inspirational figures and as 'born communicators'. But that is not always the case. One example is Teresa Tunnadine, who became Headteacher of The Compton School in North London in 1999, after seven years working there as a deputy head.

"When I came here it was a Fresh Start school, a school that had very much failed and been closed by the local authority and was being reopened. I was one of two deputies appointed by the head setting up the new school. It was very exciting. I loved it. The school grew and became very successful. We had an outstanding Ofsted. The head then left and I hadn't really thought I necessarily wanted to be in headship at all. But I decided to apply because I thought somebody might come in and unpick some of the work that we had done together."

What almost deterred her from moving into headship was the worry that she felt she did not have the communication skills to be successful.

"It put me off becoming a head. Becoming a deputy head was my aspiration from early on but I thought I would never want to stand up in an assembly with 1,000 children staring at me or talk at an open evening in front of 2,000 parents. There is no way I would have done that 15 years ago. I am not a natural orator. I'm not a head who is a big, charismatic personality. I'm much more ordinary, so it really put me off. I thought I could do every other aspect of the job; it was just this I couldn't do. I decided I would bite the bullet and get some training, get some help from people in the school who were good at it. I have become better at speaking at big set pieces. I still, for open evenings, have a friend from the media who comes in and does some coaching with myself and the children and looks at the content and method of delivery. I can still do better and will do it better next year.

"One-to-one communication is absolutely fine and I find it enjoyable. I'm very good within the school context, with my senior team, middle leadership team. It requires different styles and the ability to reflect really. It comes from experience and you develop the ability to be different when you are speaking one-to-one and when you are speaking to a big group of parents. It's just a case of doing it. Some people will take to it and it will be a huge strength for them. I've come to it through practice, and more practice and more practice."

Her message that you can learn to become an effective communicator will encourage many teachers and middle leaders who aspire to headship but may lack the confidence to take on the public role that school leadership requires. The essential attribute is to be able to communicate and connect with individuals and small groups and to believe in and be true to your values and vision for the school. Maggie Farrar's point that great communicators are skilled in "the power of conversation" is similar to the message given to print journalists when learning their craft: always write as though you are holding a conversation with your readers. The same principle applies when speaking at:

- an open evening
- in assembly
- on radio
- on television.

Your audience may be large but, in essence, you are simply having a conversation.

Even so, the complexities of running a school can make communications daunting. A modern school invariably uses a variety of methods to communicate internally with staff and pupils and externally with parents and the wider community. These include:

- newsletters
- websites
- letters
- emails
- texts
- prospectuses.

A growing number of schools and academies are employing public relations and marketing officers and are increasingly employing modern communication tools such as Twitter and video prospectuses to project and celebrate their core values, achievements and plans.

Being open and accessible

All of these things are important, says Kenny Frederick, Principal of George Green's School in East London which, among other things, publishes a weekly newsletter to keep pupils and parents informed and to celebrate achievements. What matters most, however, is to be open and accessible and a visible presence in the school corridors and classrooms.

> "There is no one way of doing it. The best thing is to be out there talking to people and that's why having an open door so that people can come in and talk to you is important. We use email, though a lot of people don't read them. We use briefings, team meetings and all sorts of things. It's always the hardest thing and the bigger the school the harder it is. It's important to be approachable. If someone wishes to see me they don't need to make an appointment days in advance. I always say 'Come into my office the door's open'. If the door's shut, I'm in a confidential meeting."

Dame Joan McVittie has witnessed the disastrous consequences for some school leaders who have failed to recognise the importance of good communication.

"It's absolutely critical and many of the heads that I've seen fail are poor communicators. It is critical that you constantly reinforce your belief in people; that you talk to them; that you know about their families. I have watched people really go to the ground because they've not been able to take the team with them. They don't communicate. They don't see it as important. They think the head's some distant figure who has to be lonely and that to me is a load of rubbish. I've never felt lonely as a head."

Having the confidence to play the part of headteacher is one of the keys to being a good communicator, but there is much more to it than that, says Teresa Tunnadine.

> "It's also about being a listener. It's about being approachable, it's about body language. It's about people knowing that you are fair and open and reasonable, empathic and sympathetic and that you won't make snap decisions unless you have to. It's about being honest and saying, 'Look, this is the way it is' so people don't have to second guess what you're thinking. It's about giving your staff lots of time to take on ideas. If the argument is strong it will be won

– that is such a useful phrase that I always keep in my head. If I can't persuade somebody to do something then it must be that the argument is wrong or that I have not articulated it properly. If that happens I have to go back and ask myself, 'Is the argument right? Maybe it isn't? Maybe they are right?' That has stood me in really good stead.

"I don't dictate at all how we're going to do things because I can't be the only person that knows the answer. The argument must be strong and I've stuck to that and it's worked through all the huge changes that have happened because I've taken staff with me."

This provides a useful checklist of the complex communication skills needed by a modern school leader. Perhaps the most important is the ability to persuade other people to buy into a particular vision or course of action.

Inspiring and motivating

Kenny Frederick puts it this way: "Leadership is about getting people to do things sometimes that perhaps they would rather not do. It's that persuasiveness, about persuading them to do even more work or to develop an idea. That's the essence of leadership, so that people want to do something and they want to develop, rather than feel they are being coerced into it. You don't get the best of people by coercion – and I know because I've worked in a climate of fear myself in the past and it's certainly not good. It can really stop you in your tracks."

In part, this ability is about inspiring and motivating people – much like the ancient Scandinavian story-teller on the eve of a battle. It is also about enabling people and giving them confidence, Frederick says.

"I think perhaps enabling is one of my strengths. One thing I'm very good at is seeing people's potential and drawing them out and giving them the confidence to try. Teachers aren't naturally confident people. They might be in their own classrooms but if you try to talk to them about going on to leadership they need to be encouraged and developed. In our school we have been really good at developing leaders at all levels."

Getting people to do things and to go that extra mile lies at the heart of good leadership. An important aspect is to be clear about what you are trying to achieve and make people feel their ideas and efforts are valued.

"Persuasion is actually about getting people to agree with your vision. You have to be able to persuade them that actually your vision is something that they believe in also. I'm a great believer in drip-feeding something and making people think that they'd thought of it themselves. It's really important to persuade people to sign up to your vision of what you want to achieve and to make sure they understand it and what their part is. By the same token when you are trying to persuade people to work harder in order to achieve something that's really hard, it's important that they understand why they are doing it and why it's important," says Frederick.

Catherine Paine, Executive Headteacher of Mount Street Academy and Saxilby Church of England Primary School in Lincolnshire, also believes in the benefits of drip-feeding ideas.

"Whenever you go into a school that is having difficulty – or in any school context – there will be those people for whom your message will immediately chime with what they already believe. So a proportion of the staff will automatically be on board with you. There is another proportion that needs to be persuaded. It's about drip-feeding that vision into absolutely everything and giving feedback to people. I am really rigorous about giving feedback to the staff. I will always respond in person, even though I'm an executive head – we are also a teaching school and have got many irons in the fire.

"My heads of school will email me a log of everything that's happened during the day. I will then go into it, whatever context I'm in, and find the people that are responsible for things that have gone well and feed back to them how what they have done has contributed to the vision. Sometimes people who might have been hovering on the edge of 'Am I into this or aren't I?' can be brought round and though they might not realise it they are actually living out the vision. It's about holding a mirror up to them really and saying, 'What you are doing is making a contribution to the vision'.

"And then of course there's a small minority of staff who won't sign up and then it's about taking whatever action that you feel is necessary in the fullness of time. We won't tolerate people who are blocking and will tell them: 'If you're not on board this train you risk being left behind and that will not be a very comfortable place to be.' It's about being quite fearless in confronting people who are working against the vision for the school and therefore against the needs of the children."

The power of persuasion

Mike Kent, who retired as Headteacher of Comber Grove Primary School in Camberwell, South London in 2012, after 31 years of headship, is a strong believer in the power of persuasion.

"I believe in persuasion far more than I believe in being autocratic. If there's something I want to change or do we will have a staff meeting about it. Everyone will have their say. We will thrash a problem out and then decide on a way to go. I will go whatever way 70 per cent of the staff want because then you'll get the other 30 per cent who will come along anyway. Occasionally that has led to meeting after meeting. I could say to the staff, 'Now this is what we're going to do and that's the way it's going to be' and many heads do. But that doesn't give teachers any kind of ownership of the problem and so I would rather spend three staff meetings thrashing it out.

"Sometimes they end up getting bored and say, 'Oh god, do what you want', so you end up doing what you wanted to do in the first place. But most of the time, two-thirds of the staff will say 'Yes, this is the way we should go' and mostly the rest will come on board. The great prize is that people won't wander round muttering about it and say we shouldn't have done this. They will know it's a consensus. If people understand a decision and think it's sensible, then they will make it work."

Authoritarian line

Llyn Codling, Executive Headteacher of Portswood and St Mary's Church of England primary schools in Southampton, takes a somewhat different view. While persuasiveness is an important quality, there are times when leaders need to take a more authoritarian line, she says.

"If you've built up a great team and you've all got the same vision and drive and you've got that same relentless focus on teaching then there's not that much persuasion needed. However when you go into a school that you've got to move on, there are some bits where you've got to be didactic and there are some bits where you need to be persuasive. Sometimes, yes, you've got to be really authoritarian saying, 'Sorry this is non-negotiable'. It sounds awful, but when you're trying to shift a school from unsatisfactory to good there are some things, like good teaching, that are not negotiable at all. That is what everyone should be doing."

Ani Magill, Headteacher of St John the Baptist School in Woking, Surrey, firmly believes in the importance of effective communication but echoes Maggie Farrar's suspicion of school leaders who see it as a one-way process. What matters, she says, is not the message delivered by the school leadership, but the response it receives.

"Effective communication is a two-way thing. What we need to ask is: how do we know we are doing a good job as leaders? How do we know we're communicating well? At St John the Baptist, we have lots of ways that we try to improve and find out if there's any way that we're not communicating very well and, as a result, make sure we change. For example, if you go to a staff meeting there will be a paper on your chair and everybody will write down one thing that would make their job easier, or write down one way that communication can be improved. Or you might be asked to write down three things the leadership team can do to improve; that type of thing. We also try to do a lot of it in one-to-ones and verbal feedback, rather than hiding behind emails and bits of paper."

The ability to listen

No matter how persuasive a headteacher or principal is, they also need to be able to listen and make time to sit down with people and work things through together, says Magill.

"It's that two-to-one – two ears and one mouth – and really trying to make sure you listen to people. When people ask, 'Have you got a minute?' they mean 'Have you got a minute to listen to me?' not, 'Have you got a minute *to* talk to me?' We do 360 degree feedback for everybody, including me, and one of the things that came back in the early days was that a few members of staff said, 'Don't think that you've always got to have the answers, sometimes we just want you to listen'. I used to think that when people came to me that I had to find an answer for them, but it's just that people want to be listened to. And by verbally articulating what's on their mind, it often solves the problem, because they can see themselves what to do."

Many successful leaders stress the importance of being a good listener. While the ability to persuade people to sign up to your vision can be crucial, the art of good leadership is to treat every interaction as a two-way conversation. It is not just a case of being the person who shouts the loudest, says Dame Joan McVittie.

"Listening is a critical skill. Coming from a big family as I do, with four sisters and a brother, you can imagine we always had to talk very loud and very fast to get a hearing. I had a lot of training from the National College in developing listening skills because I think that was a skill I needed to work on and it really helped me."

Roger Pope, Principal of Kingsbridge Community College in Devon, says: "On a one-to-one basis you can win an awful lot of people over if you show you are actively listening – if they come away feeling that you have understood them."

Madeleine Vigar, Principal of The Castle Partnership Academy Trust in Haverhill, Suffolk, says that the ability to listen to people enables leaders to gauge the impact of what they are doing and make adjustments if necessary.

"Listening is important because you have to take the temperature of your school. You can't just go out there and say, 'This is how I want it'. You have to have your antennae out, you have to go out and see where people are at. You have got to check because if people are off message then it's very clear that in order to run a successful school you have to have everyone singing from the same hymn sheet. So you have to listen as a leader.

"It's about taking the temperature of an organisation and adjusting, because you have to be flexible. There are methods of school improvement where they say, 'Right this is how you improve a school – use this model and go out there and do it'. I don't believe that's the way you improve a school. I think you've got to go in with a simple vision, do your analysis of where the school is at and then move with the staff and the children, bringing them with you. The job we've done at Castle Manor has been about bringing people with us."

Lynn Slinger, Headteacher of Forest Way Special School in Coalville, Leicestershire, is also aware of the dangers for leaders who talk well but don't listen.

"I think to communicate well you have got to be a good listener. It becomes harder the bigger an organisation becomes. When I first came to Forest Way there were between 20 and 30 staff. Now we have 113 at the last count. You are never going to be able to communicate as well with a larger number. You have to make sure you have very clear systems and people have still got to feel valued within that larger number, which is a challenge," she says.

Mutual understanding and trust

Good communication also depends crucially on mutual understanding and trust, says Slinger.

> "I have worked with a number of people who have been very good communicators. I think the essential thing is trust. If you trust each other everything else falls in place. Some people are better communicators than others, but without the trust you are never going to have an open relationship. To have an open relationship in which you can communicate freely you need to trust each other. I've been in professional relationships with people who are very bright, who can speak very articulately but actually I don't think we were really communicating because we didn't trust each other. So although I feel communication is very important I think it needs to be underpinned by trust."

Managing communications in a large school can be particularly challenging. It is important that the headteacher deals sensitively and caringly with people's concerns, says Sue Hargadon, Principal of Farlingaye High School, a comprehensive in Suffolk with over 1,900 students.

"If you look at most of the times when you go wrong with your staff and parents, it's often due to poor communication. When I get a message from a parent usually what they are cross about isn't that something has happened, it's because no-one has bothered to get back to them. Maybe they have got unrealistic expectations about things but often the problem is because you or your staff didn't stop and think about how you said something or you got somebody else to do something and it would have been better coming from you. To run a successful big school, communication is vital."

Involving the staff

While a headteacher needs to be a confident, persuasive communicator and a good listener they also need to involve staff and other stakeholders in major decisions affecting their school. It is important to give them ownership of changes that affect them, says Patricia Scott, Headteacher of St Luke's High School in Barrhead, East Renfrewshire in Scotland.

"You can't do it all yourself. You have got to set up structures so that you have distributed leadership, in which everyone has a voice and feels that they have an ownership in the decision-making and within school. We've just completed a huge consultation exercise, as we do every year, on the school improvement plan which involves people at every level – staff, pupils, parents, and all our major partners. If they are given a say at an early stage they are more likely to support it. By giving them the opportunity to reflect and say what things they think are going really well and where we need to go to next it enables us to gather all the evidence together.

"That is something which I think is really powerful. It enables you to then say: 'Well, this is what you are telling us, these are the key areas that are coming through, so how are we going to take this forward?' So I think that persuasion has to go hand in hand with people feeling true ownership about the improvement of the school and a responsibility for the part that they have to play. They need to feel that they will be listened to and that their opinion will be sought and acted upon. It's that active involvement element of it that's really important – listening to the pupil voice, the staff voice and the parent voice in a genuine way."

Catherine Paine also believes in the benefits of involving staff, parents and pupils. As a National Leader of Education (NLE) who gives advice and support to leaders working in challenging circumstances, she also warns of the dangers of going into a school with a fixed plan or off-the-shelf strategy.

"You need to remember that expediency might get you instant results but it doesn't help you win hearts and minds. There are many situations where I know quite clearly what it is that's got to be done but I canvass staff views and consult and meet parents and children. I engage with the staff to generate their views on how particular issues should be tackled. One of two things happens: either they come up with all the things that I was hoping they would do, in which case we've got a 'win'; or they come up with things that are better than what I thought of in the first place.

"Never yet have I found myself thinking they are way off course and having to introduce something that is an autocratic decision. The long-term view sometimes means that it takes longer but at the end of it you have a community of people who are with you rather than people who are going through the motions of rubber-stamping what you have forced on them and whose hearts and minds aren't in it. As an NLE, you are always trying to work towards an endgame, which is that a school is able to stand on its own two feet without you. Expediency won't work because as soon as you are gone they will just revert back. These things have to become engrained in people."

Self-awareness

Roger Pope says that leaders need to be aware of their own strengths and weaknesses and cover for any shortcomings by appointing someone on their staff with strengths in those areas. Being able to draw on good communication skills is vital, he says.

"I'm very aware of the fact that I've got an English background, that I'm an extravert and that I can do all of that communication very well. I know that my logical data type brain is not that strong, so I make sure that I've got people on my team who can do those bits. I think that where you've got heads who are very good on the logical mathematical side of things, but not so good on the communication then I think they can struggle to get their ideas over to people.

"I think that you have to be a top communicator in terms of your written skills because a lot of stuff that you put out is in print. I also think it is very important to be able to take an audience with you because if a group of staff sit in front of the head for ten minutes and then go away bored then they are going to go away and chunter. That undermines the head's 'institutional trust'."

A media profile

One of the benefits of having exceptional communication skills is that it can help your school gain a higher profile through the local and, on occasions, national media. Roger Pope writes regularly about education and leadership for the *TES* (Times Educational Supplement). Geoff Barton, Headteacher of King Edward VI School in Bury St Edmunds, also writes for the *TES* and frequently appears on radio and television locally and nationally.

When Bernard Trafford took up his current post as Headmaster of the Royal Grammar School, Newcastle, in 2008, one of his priorities was to raise the school profile. As a leading light in the Headmasters' and

Headmistresses' Conference who also writes for the national media he was able to secure a weekly column in the local press, providing valuable publicity for the school.

Mike Kent became a *TES* columnist and one of its most popular writers after successfully challenging what he describes as "a very difficult and very aggressive Ofsted inspection" in 2000. His determination to fight a public battle over what he saw as an unjust process resulted in a powerful feature article which prompted several other leaders who felt their schools had been unfairly treated to make formal complaints about the same Ofsted team. The inspectors' judgement about Comber Grove was subsequently overturned, vindicating Kent's action.

One of the hallmarks of his regular *TES* columns, which have been running for more than a decade, is that they tell the story of what it is like to lead a South London primary school. They describe the joys of the job of working with children, wryly celebrate the children's achievements, praise the staff and poke fun at the bureaucracy and regulation that form part and parcel of a headteacher's life.

Kenny Frederick is another high profile headteacher who writes regularly for both the national and local media and frequently appears on television and radio to speak about issues that affect her school. She sees it as a moral duty for school leaders to stand up for their pupils, staff, parents and community. They also have a responsibility to play an active part in the debate over the future of education, she says.

"We have a duty to stand up and be counted. In the days when government used to properly consult I would get involved in Department for Education discussions and focus groups and things like that and try to be part of the solution and part of the policy-making process rather than always be negative. I would rather be 'done with' than 'done to'."

Sometimes, she says, awkward things need to be said and she has been an outspoken critic of government policy on occasions. But her outlook is always positive and she has no time for negativity.

"I'm happy to help develop policy, to be consulted and to give my views and to give up my time. I've done that at all sorts of different levels and I think it's important to encourage my staff to do the same, even though it takes a bit of time. You can't just be a moaner. Sometimes it's easier for a long-term head like me to say something than it is for somebody else.

"I remember when I was first appointed, sitting in heads' meetings, where you didn't really know what was going on. Some of the older heads would just say 'Well, you get on with learning the business'. But you have a responsibility as you get more experienced to take on a bit more and to be more vocal. When you first become a head you haven't got the chance to do that and are just trying to keep your head above the water. But I do think it's important that you do fight back in the media and that's why I'm involved in the National Association of Head Teachers. Otherwise you just get trampled on."

Richard Harman, Headmaster of Uppingham School, Rutland, is another leader who believes the job requires great communication skills at all levels. "Whether with pupils, staff, parents, press, alumni, visitors, the local community, you need to be able to deliver in writing and in person, set-pieces and off-the-cuff talks alike," he says.

"That was the thing that surprised me most when I first became a head, the constant need to communicate. Every day you are likely to be standing up talking to a group of people or presenting 'the vision'. You are hosting more or less everything in your school. Even if you are not actually hosting it you are the presiding officer. You need to be able to turn your hand to that at any minute and just the sheer constancy of that was quite a challenge in the beginning.

"You can never be a good enough communicator. There's always going to be somebody who feels you haven't consulted them. And that's particularly true in this world of websites, blogging and social media. You have to be as up with the game as you can – and keep humble because you will never get it completely right."

8

Curiosity

Successful school leaders are outward-looking and curious. They are excellent networkers, great opportunists and in touch with events.

One of the dangers of leading a school is becoming inward-looking and getting caught up in your own internal problems and concerns. Successful headteachers and principals avoid this in many different ways. One is by having wide outside interests and, as John Newton, Headmaster of Taunton School in Somerset puts it, keeping "intellectually fresh". It may be by reading widely or taking an interest in the arts or singing in a choir. Perhaps more important is to stay in touch with current events and be on top of issues – both local and national – that are likely to have an impact on your school or open up new opportunities.

Keeping in touch

The best school leaders, in the words of Mike Kent, former Headteacher of Comber Grove Primary School in Camberwell, South London, have "a good knowledge of everything that's currently happening in education". This helps them to predict events and shape the future, keeping their schools on the right side of developments and able to take advantage of the latest research. They are also great opportunists. "Don't miss opportunities, as long as they fit within your overall vision: keep your wits about you and think tactically as well as strategically", is how Richard Harman, Headmaster of Uppingham School in Rutland puts it.

Networking is a crucial skill employed by successful heads. "Networking is teambuilding on a larger scale. It opens up opportunities through chance meetings and conversations which grow to bigger things. It also enables us to gain an alternative vision and thereby to circumvent and overcome obstacles," says Andrew Fleck, Headmaster of Sedbergh School in Cumbria.

For the most successful heads, things happen because of their ability to see beyond their own schools and grasp any opportunity to compare what other heads are doing with their own practice. "You cannot take a school to new levels if you are insular," says Roger Pope, Principal of Kingsbridge Community College in Devon.

Alison Peacock is Headteacher of The Wroxham School in Potters Bar, Hertfordshire, which has gained an international reputation for its inclusive, creative approach to school improvement in the primary sector. She is also National Network Leader of the Cambridge Primary Review (CPR) which between 2007 and 2009 carried out the most comprehensive enquiry into English primary education since the Plowden Report in the 1960s. In this role, she continues to play an influential role disseminating the CPR's research, engaging in policy development and debates and building a professional network of primary education practitioners. As such, she speaks regularly at conferences and seminars and comes into contact with primary teachers from all over the country.

This professional engagement has a powerful role to play in helping primary teachers and school leaders draw strength from each other and find a collective voice, she says.

"I will give you an example. I was at a conference in Brighton and I gave a speech. At the end a guy came up to me, he was a deputy head and he was in tears. He said, 'You have just reminded me why I came into teaching'. I think we need reminding about what it is that we set out to do because there are so many pressures on the profession, which are about outputs. Actually our job is about children and children will attain more highly when they are engaged and valued and loved for who they are and also challenged and given high quality teaching.

"So I think my role of working with the CPR network is about helping people to connect with each other to build that professional courage. Let's hold onto the things that really matter. Sometimes people are in adverse circumstances and that makes holding onto what really matters tricky. If there is someone down the road who you can phone up, or if there is a website you can go on, or a lecture you can go to or a book you can read, that helps you keep on track.

"That's what needs to happen, I think particularly within primary education. At the moment the policy is dominated by secondary education and politicians tend only to talk about secondary schools. Primary education is at a very different, crucial stage in its own right and we need a really strong emphasis on what works in primary education. I feel as though I'm taking on that role a lot of the time and I'm happy to do that if it encourages teachers to go back into school and think suddenly, 'There's a rainbow in the sky, I can go and show the children the rainbow'. If they start to develop a bit more courage about what really matters then maybe we will have more children who can experience that kind of thing."

A culture of enquiry

Peacock speaks passionately of the need to engage children in their learning and to re-engage the teaching profession by building a culture of enquiry. In order to do this teachers and school leaders need to be able to break out of their everyday routines, she says.

"It is imperative that we remind ourselves about what works in terms of learning when we are working with adults. It's patently obvious that a staff meeting on a Monday night for an hour at the end of a long day with a cup of tea and a dry biscuit is hardly going to be the best place to enable new thinking to happen. We don't have weekly staff meetings because it's just not a good time for active learning. There are all sorts of alternatives and I think sometimes we treat ourselves quite badly as a profession. We work very hard, we blame ourselves for everything, we let other people blame us for everything and we forget that in order to nurture children's learning we need to nurture ourselves. It's no wonder that teachers become demoralised because the job is always going to be impossible; it's a question of how you find a way through it.

"There are many school leaders that fall into the trap of thinking, 'If I gather my staff together into a room and tell them stuff for an hour they will then go and do it'. There's no evidence that works whatsoever. It's much more important to build a culture of enquiry within the school where people are seeking to ask questions about their own practice, where they want to read, to engage and discuss things not because they have been told they have got to do it but because they are excited about learning."

New ideas and opportunities

School leaders have a critical role to play in ensuring their institutions do not become isolated from the outside world, whether the local community or further afield. They need to be attuned to new ideas and opportunities that might benefit their schools and use their position to take full advantage, says Andrew Fleck.

"Part of my role is to be a conduit of ideas into the school, a conduit of people into the school. I have a responsibility to use my authority as Headmaster of Sedbergh for the benefit of my pupils. That might be by bringing in speakers and forging relations that might bring them opportunities. The other reason that being outward-looking is so important is that if I am able to create an enthusiastic staff who want to develop things then they are going to come into my office with good ideas and I have to be attuned to what's going on around the school, because it would be very easy to say, 'Oh no, I've seen that before 20 years ago, we're not going to do that', or jump on a bandwagon which perhaps doesn't lead anywhere. So I think one has to be attuned to what's going on elsewhere."

Fleck is keen to stress the connection between the headteacher's team-building role within the school and his or her responsibility to build alliances and connections beyond the school gates. The head has a duty to be highly visible and engaged with pupils and staff in the classrooms and school corridors. He or she needs to find time to connect with people both inside and outside school and should never become bogged down doing routine tasks.

"If I spend my whole time doing admin my teachers might rightly assume that I think that admin is the most important thing. It goes back to empathy. If I am catching people doing things well then I can offer my support and congratulations. They know that I know what they are doing and the level of commitment they are putting in. There's nothing more energising than your boss seeing you doing something you are proud of. That's why I'm out there. And the same is true of pupils.

"The most powerful force in a school is the pupil body and if I as a head – and I have done in the past at my previous school – galvanise the pupils quite deliberately into a certain direction of change, rather than the staff, then the staff have no choice. If the pupils are asking, demanding, encouraging and enthused about something the staff will naturally follow. I can't do that without talking to the children and so I have lunch with them, go into lessons, see them in the corridors and go running with them. It's all about living it with them. It's important to reflect that because Sedbergh is a 24/7 boarding school. If they see me in my running tights or my jeans then my authority is not in any way undermined because they intuitively know that I'm a human being and not some form of management robot."

One school leader with a high profile on the national education scene is Geoff Barton, Headteacher of King Edward VI School in Bury St Edmunds, Suffolk. As a regular contributor to *TES*, author of textbooks and resources for English teachers and an energetic social networker and blogger, he has unusually wide interests. It is these extra-curricular activities that help him to stay fresh and engaged with the profession, he says.

Long-term commitment

Even so, he remains deeply committed to his school and local community and has little time for heads who take on schools as a short-term project with no intention of staying for the long haul. He made his own intentions clear when he took up his present headship, his first, in 2002.

"I remember saying to the staff, somewhat arrogantly, when I got it: 'I'm not going to do this as a short-term fix, I'm going to be here at least ten years'. I can't quite think why I said that, but I think it was partly because I had seen people who regarded headship as a feat of plate-spinning where they would start spinning the plates at one school and then they would rush off somewhere else and start spinning another plate. The thing that interests me about headship is not really the stage where you get things started. It's the later, deeper, harder stuff where you are really trying to make an impact on the school culture.

"There are things that we did eight years ago where we are now really starting to see the benefits like, for example, our emphasis on student leadership. I think there's a real satisfaction in that long-term process. I also think that communities need people to stick around a bit more, rather than appearing to be jumping from one job to another," he says.

Barton is able to make time for his own outside interests partly by working long hours but also by being ruthlessly focused on what he thinks is important, rather than getting bogged down in the minutiae of the job. It is about being proactive rather than reactive, he says.

"I think I probably learned early on, when I was head of English, that the nice thing about being given a leadership role is that you can pick and choose a bit what you do and don't want to do. One of the things that I'm not very good at is paperwork and so I avoid doing it as much as I can. I sit and do the post every day with my PA and I literally throw away 70 per cent. It goes straight into the bin to protect my staff. There will be some heads that spend lots of time reacting to things that they probably think are important, like surveys. We get about five or six of them a day and they all go in the bin. That clears the way for me to do the stuff I am more interested in – which is usually working directly with staff and students."

Potential opportunities

Making outside connections and being alive to potential opportunities can be hugely beneficial and can also help sustain a school leader over a long career, Barton says.

"I very quickly realised that by getting involved on a local level it created opportunities in the school. I am on the board of Bid for Bury, which is a kind of town centre management group. I'm also on a charitable board for Ipswich Town Football Club. Now some people would say, 'What on earth are you doing on those kinds of things?' But what I think it has done is that it's got the school on the map in some very useful places. It also, incredibly frequently, creates opportunities for our youngsters. For example, someone will say, 'Could your choir come and sing at this?' or, 'Have you some students who would like to do that?' It's the power of networking.

"I think that is something I've really learned over the past ten years and I now realise it is an absolutely key part of the job. Partly, I think, it's developed because of my interest in the bigger issues. As head of English I was always pontificating on the future of English in the *TES* and in writing journals. Technology has also made it easier to communicate more widely about those issues. You suddenly find yourself on Twitter having conversations with policy advisers who have the ear of Michael Gove, the Education Secretary. I think in some ways that has been one of the areas that has been fascinating to me and it's got me into conversations with people at a national and increasingly international level.

"All of these things, I think, are to the advantage of our youngsters. It's also been helpful on a personal level. They have kept me refreshed and interested. I think that what has motivated me throughout my career has never been ambition. It's boredom, fear of boredom, and I've always liked the fact that I could take on some new project."

The most successful school leaders are opportunists, always ready to grasp chances that will benefit their school, says Richard Harman.

"As the Bible says, you need to be 'wise as serpents, innocent as doves' [Matthew 10:16-20]. It's about being double-faced without being two-faced; keeping your integrity but still being open to opportunities. You do need to be a tactician – to be able to keep an eye out for the chance that will come your way, the open goal that you mustn't miss – even while you are giving the grand vision. It can sometimes be a messy business and you have to be prepared to roll your sleeves up and take opportunities as they come, whether business opportunities, educational or media ones, or whatever they may be.

"Your job is to look ahead. People can say, 'We are fine as we are', but if you don't look ahead you are in trouble. You need to be out there looking at what's happening nationally, internationally, being in other schools, in other forums and networking. It's also important for one's own leadership development to network with other people who aren't school leaders because if you only meet other school leaders that in itself can sometimes be an insular thing. You can really learn from leaders in other spheres, whether in business, the military, the church or wherever. To keep yourself nimble and on your toes you have to get the exercise, get out there and keep networking."

Being open to ideas and influences from outside the school can make a critical difference, says Dame Joan McVittie, Headteacher of Woodside High School in Wood Green, North London.

"One way that schools can totally destroy themselves is if you get a headteacher who pulls up the drawbridge and just doesn't look at what's out there, communicate with others and share skills, resources, teachers. I would go mad if I had to sit in a school all the time. Being open to what is happening elsewhere has helped my school hugely. I've been on the governing council for the National College for School Leadership and when they say they are going to pilot something I will say 'I'll try it for you'. I've done a lot of things over the years with the Youth Sports Trust and we were then successful with our bid to become the hub for a youth sports co-ordinator programme. It's by developing out-of-school contacts that you become aware of what's out there and that helps you to enrich school life for the kids."

Finding the right balance

While being open to outside influences is important, headteachers need to find the right balance between being a hands-on leader and spending time away from school. This is especially true for new heads, says Ani Magill, Headteacher of St John the Baptist School in Woking, Surrey.

"I think that when people start headship they cannot be outward-looking because it's so overwhelming to get from day to day. But I think that once you've started to get the school where you want it to be it's really important that you are seeing what's out there the whole time, learning from the best and networking with other schools.

"It's a case of finding the right balance, of networking but not being out of school too often. But if you want your own school to improve you've got to go and see the best schools around. We go on tour every year to the best schools in the country. Two of us would go and then come back and tell the rest of the team how we can improve as a result of what we've seen."

Even for a newly-appointed head it can be a huge advantage having a network of practitioners and friends that you can rely on for support and advice, says Lynn Slinger, Headteacher of Forest Way Special School in Coalville, Leicestershire.

"That has been one of my biggest sources of strength. When I came into this school I was lucky because I already worked in Leicestershire and I had a network of colleagues that were in senior leadership roles who gave me the emotional support and help I needed early on. The special school heads' group, my local heads' group and also the local authority, which has been very supportive as well, have been the major influences on me in terms of networking and sharing good practice and sharing experience. How you would ever achieve success without that I don't know. I certainly couldn't do it because you learn so much from others and you can help each other as well.

"As a National Teaching School, something we've recently taken on, we are part of an alliance of schools. Some schools within our alliance need a lot of support at the moment but they will be helping other schools at a certain stage as well. If you've got that network you can balance each other's need depending on what is happening at the time. So I think networking is really crucial, including at a national level, something which in the past I might have been a bit sniffy about. It can bring a lot of benefits to a school. Local networking is absolutely essential, but if you can also get into a national network – the National Teaching School Alliance is a really good way of doing that – that can add another dimension. It really helps a school to develop."

Slinger recognises there are potential dangers in a leader being out of school too often. It is imperative, when you are not in school, to be able to depend on your senior team, she says.

"I have seen some really good schools where the head has been out so much and they've had an inspection, the school has gone under and the head has lost their job. It also depends on the team that you have in your school. I've got a deputy who could have been a head who is a very safe pair of hands to leave this school in. When she retires I will have to look at what I'm doing and make sure I am in school more. I am quite careful about being out of school too much. Headteachers who are very measured do this. At different times in their school's lives they say, 'I'm sorry I can't come out much at the moment because of these weaknesses that need to be addressed'. A good head has got to be able to spot those times."

An outward-facing culture

While it is important to reach beyond your school and to have good networking skills there are dangers for any leader who spends too much time away from their primary role. It is far more important to cultivate an outward-facing culture among your pupils and staff, says Andrew Hutchinson, Executive Principal of Parkside Federation Academies in Cambridge.

"The model that I work on is to encourage my students and staff to be outward-looking. I like to make sure that a lot of the ideas and development have come from within the senior team or at middle leadership level. It is far more important to me to encourage them to be outward-looking than for me to be the one who's always out there doing all the networking and all the other stuff. I think the culture of a school needs to be outward-looking and the leader needs to model that culture. It shouldn't reside within the leader.

"There is a danger that you can become detached. There are only a limited number of hours in the day and as a leader you need for the majority of those hours to be routed in the organisation itself. You need to be experiencing the day-to-day life of the school and focusing on the detail. I would give far more weight to the need to focus on the detail of everyday life than I would to the need to be outward facing. It's important to be able to understand your context and to network and to get ideas from other people and other schools, but first and foremost you've got to understand what your own organisation is like.

Mike Kent is another who warns against headteachers spending too much time away from school.

"It happens with quite a lot of people. I know my staff appreciate that I'm in school because if there's a difficulty they get it resolved. Having said that, I am invited to talk to various heads and that can be fascinating because it can be in a different part of the country and as far away from the inner-city where I work as it can possibly be. You get their take on primary education and it can be very different to the problems that I have. But I don't tend to go to local meetings so much. It's very easy for meetings to become talking shops.

"There are some heads that actually like being out of their schools and you can easily become a professional meeting-attender. I can think of a guy and his school was very good until he started running the local teachers' association. Because that took up so much of his time he was often out of his school. His school then failed its Ofsted and fell apart. He retired a very bitter man. There's a danger of taking your eye off the ball."

Despite his reputation as a hands-on practitioner whose regular *TES* columns focus on the everyday situations and issues facing schools, Kent says it is important to keep abreast of the latest ideas and developments. The best ideas and innovations can have a huge influence on your school, while others may simply be fads and should be rejected.

"I started teaching back in the days of Plowden and in those days the expectations of what you should do in a primary classroom was very different compared with what is happening now. We have always steered a central course at Comber Grove. There are things children have to do. They have to learn to read and write and to add up and we've never veered off that central road. But equally, you're always interested to take on new things that you think are exciting. Look at ICT and the way that's snowballed over the years. We were one of the first schools in London to have BBC Micros [one of the first educational computer systems] in school. We had one in every classroom and that was quite unique at the time. I felt that was a great benefit.

"As you go through your career as a head there are things that you think are a really good idea – science, cookery, modern languages. All these things we have brought in and which are very strong components of the national curriculum. It's very beneficial. You've got to look at what's out there and what's available. But equally you have got to reject things that you don't think are going to work in your school."

Farlingaye High School in Suffolk is one of over 300 high-performing schools in England that are members of the Leading Edge Partnership Programme run by the Specialist Schools and Academies Trust. Schools in the network are dedicated to sharing practice and working with other schools to raise achievement. Farlingaye's Principal, Sue Hargadon, says the programme provides the opportunity for her and other members of her team to go into other schools and share ideas.

"That is one of the most powerful things we do. We also work as a leading edge group of headteachers in Suffolk, which I run. That idea of sharing ideas and being curious about what other people do, combined with the enthusiasm it generates to implement them or adapt them to your own school, is just fantastic," she says.

Education policy

For an increasing number of successful school leaders, this ability to look outwards means grasping opportunities to forge partnerships with other schools, converting to academies and intervening to help and support other schools that are struggling. It is in this area of education where the biggest and most controversial changes are taking place. This is especially the case in England, where more than half of state-funded secondary schools have converted to academies, cutting ties with their local authorities whose future role in state education is now in doubt.

The creation of a national system of academies, initially in the secondary sector but with primary schools likely to follow over the next decade, has huge implications for school and college leaders and underlines the need to be outward-looking and forward thinking. This emerging landscape is being shaped by new networks and partnerships such as academy chains, federations and umbrella trusts. It includes private and voluntary sector providers, partners and sponsors as well as independent partnerships of like-minded or geographically-connected schools.

The broad vision of this new national system appears to be shared, by and large, by each of the three major political parties. It reflects a shift towards autonomous schools that are accountable to central government by means of performance measures and periodic inspection that began with the 1988 Education Reform Act. Beneath this broad consensus, however, there are deep ideological divisions about future education policy. The fundamental dividing lines are between those who would like to see a deregulated market for schools in which providers are able to operate at a profit and those who believe schools should work together in partnership rather than competition – and not for profit. This debate is likely to continue in the years to come with political compromise and 'triangulation' policies preventing governments of either right or left from going to extremes.

As increasing numbers of primary and secondary schools opt for greater autonomy and become academies or free schools there may well be a new role for local government with the creation of school commissioners. The new networks of schools and academies are also encouraging collaboration, seeking economies of scale by sharing administration and support services and working together on staff training and leadership development.

Even so, Kenny Frederick, Principal of George Green's School in Tower Hamlets, is one of many school leaders who are concerned that this newly-evolving system could undermine co-operation between schools. It is more important than ever, she says, for headteachers to learn from and help each other, rather than become inward-looking.

"That's really important. Sometimes I get a bit worried about the way schools are closing in on themselves and there is very much a culture of not sharing. I've worked for a headteacher in the past who wouldn't share anything. I've always been a great collaborator and sharer of ideas, but she didn't like that because we were always in competition with other schools. It worries me that not so much of that happens any more, that people are closing in on themselves because of this competitive element.

"A lot of people talk about collaboration and are quite happy to take your ideas but actually give nothing back. But I go into other schools to see what they are doing. We have a collaborative group with our local primary schools that I chair. We hold our meetings in different schools, we do learning walks, share ideas and do self-review in each other's schools. You have to have that openness and trust and I don't think there's a lot of that around in the secondary sector. It's a big shame because I want my school to succeed but not at the expense of another school. I want us all to succeed because they are all our kids. That is not a view held by some colleagues who want to succeed but don't want the school down the road to succeed.

"That has got to change. Of course, you must be competitive to succeed in a job like this, but that is being fuelled by the education system at the moment. It's dog-eat-dog and that competitive attitude is not encouraging people to share or meet with other colleagues and develop things together."

Scotland

In marked contrast to England, the Scottish school system has moved towards a more structured collaborative model. In 2011, Learning and Teaching Scotland, which provides advice and support on teaching and the curriculum, merged with Her Majesty's Inspectorate for Education to form Education Scotland. Patricia Scott, Headteacher of St Luke's High School in Barrhead, East Renfrewshire, is strongly supportive of the new partnership approach and says it is "a much more productive model" than the old Scottish system.

"The whole approach towards inspection, although still very rigorous, is much more a model of 'inspection with' the school as opposed to 'inspection of' the school. It is very much a two-way communication, very much a dialogue. For example, the first part of the inspection comes from the headteacher and the senior leadership team who are able to say, 'This is our school, this is where we are in terms of self-evaluation. These are our strengths. These are the areas we're working on'. That has been very good for Scottish education and I think it shows real trust in the profession.

"Schools in Scotland have been using self-evaluation for many years now. But also, before we get to HMI-level of school inspection, within the local authority we have quality improvement teams. So we have different levels of working together on school improvement. We also work on a cluster basis. In my own situation, for example, we are just about to have an authority review on maths and numeracy. Last year, our cluster had a school transitions review. Each review puts the focus on a particular aspect of learning and school life. So I think we're very used to that kind of culture and working with lots of partners in terms of review and setting the improvement agenda."

Irrespective of which particular school system or context a leader operates in it is crucial that they take an interest in 'the bigger picture' and become involved, says Scott.

"You can't be insular. You have got to be very much looking at the bigger picture, at what is coming through research, what is coming onto the national agenda and what are we learning from partners. In our school we have partnerships with other European countries. It's really important to have that wider landscape in which you are really looking forward and asking questions on behalf of young people. Questions such as: 'What skills and abilities are we giving them a grounding in that is going to take them forward for the next 50 years of their life?' It's really important to be part of those kinds of discussions, to get involved in national debates and to go to places where you can have first-hand experience and contribute to that wider conversation.

"I've been involved in different groups through the Scottish government as well as headteacher forums and meetings with directorate colleagues within our own local authority. I am an Associate Assessor with HMI, or Education Scotland as it's called now, which gives me first-hand experience. I've also been involved in think-tank groups and I've presented at national conferences. So I think that to hear at first-hand what's happening and be part of the debate is very important."

London Challenge

One of the most successful school improvement programmes introduced by Tony Blair's Labour government was the London Challenge, which began in 2003 under the direction of the Commissioner for London Schools, Sir Tim Brighouse. The programme set out to raise achievement in low-performing secondary schools in the capital by establishing collaborative networks and providing support, challenge and mentoring from experienced school leaders.

By the end of the decade the programme had helped to make the capital's secondary schools the best-performing in England. In 2008, the programme was extended to primary schools and similar programmes were introduced in the country's biggest cities. In 2010, Ofsted reported that the programme had "continued to improve outcomes for pupils in London's primary and secondary schools at a faster rate than nationally".

One of the system leaders who was involved in the programme from its inception was Teresa Tunnadine, Headteacher of The Compton School in Finchley, North London. She argues that involvement in outreach work through initiatives like the London Challenge and National Teaching Schools benefited both her own school and the other schools she has worked with. Crucially, it has also kept her motivated, she says.

"It's been the case for me really since my third year of headship. I was fortunate enough to be part of Tim Brighouse's London Challenge initiative and got drawn into supporting heads in other schools. Since that time I have been involved in the wider system mentoring heads and now as a National Teaching School. It's definitely kept me in headship. I'm in headship now because headship is not what it was when I started.

"Headship is about having at least one foot outside of the school looking at what's going on elsewhere, supporting the system more widely and picking up very good ideas. Some of our best ideas we have had in our school have come from working with some of the best heads in the country. It's kept me interested. My work is very varied. I would not be in headship now otherwise.

"I have talked, as part of a research paper I did for the National College [*System leadership through extended headship roles*, National College for School Leadership, 2011], to a number of heads and they have said the same thing. The outreach work that we do means that we are kept interested and our role is varied. It means people in our schools can step up and run the school when we are not there and that's good for them and keeps them interested in turn and keeps them in the school. But it also enables us to capture all the best practice, decide what things are best for our school and bring them in. It's helped us get our results up from 50 per cent five A*–C grades at GCSE to 97 per cent over a decade with the same intake. We have got much better at what we do and that is significantly because of the good ideas that I've captured from elsewhere."

Advantages of collaboration

The advantages of being outward-facing and working with other school partners are arguably even greater for leaders in schools that are improving and aiming to achieve 'good' or 'outstanding' Ofsted grades, Tunnadine says.

"I have just been asked to run a programme across London called Securing Good for schools that are satisfactory or are not securely good. I'm going to be working with those schools and encouraging and helping heads who are at the point of now needing to break beyond their school boundaries. They've done a very good job in their own school but now need to work with other cultures beyond their school to see if they can make a difference.

"It's important for me to be providing opportunities for people to grow into the shoes of people like me who may be retiring in the next five years. Part of our role as more experienced heads is to grow the new generation of system leaders and to reinvigorate and encourage them by showing them that they can do very good work beyond their schools. It's all part of the system leadership that's going on at the moment. Teaching School alliances are one vehicle for that."

One of the driving forces encouraging schools to collaborate in order to secure improvement across the system has been the National College for School Leadership. Maggie Farrar, its former Executive Director, argues that the best school leaders and principals are generous in giving support to others.

"They are not just looking at what's in it for themselves or their school. That to me is selfish and using the system for themselves. School leadership is not a race. It must be balanced with a real commitment to help others. Investing time in helping others to improve is just as important as time invested in helping yourself and your school to improve," she says.

As a civil servant, Farrar naturally supports the policy of autonomous schools espoused by successive governments since 1988. But unless collaboration between schools continues to be strengthened there is a danger that greater independence will lead to "a fragmented, very isolated system", she says.

> "I don't have any problem with autonomy for schools if it helps them to improve and get a better deal. What I would be worried about is if that led to some schools becoming very isolated because in that case children in those schools probably would not get as good a deal as children in the other schools. That is why the College is working to set up a network of National Teaching Schools which will work in broad alliances with each other.
>
> "There are lots of other examples of schools coming together in clusters, alliances, federations and chains and that's fine. Our role is to help leaders to be as skilled as possible in collaborating, sharing excellent practice and helping each other to improve so we can genuinely move towards a self-improving school system, but one which will be made up of diverse types of school."

As this book draws to a conclusion, there is a real worry that this system of checks and balances – described by Farrar as "autonomy with collaboration" – may be overturned as some of the tectonic plates beneath its foundations begin to shift. Following the 2010 general election, the incoming Tory Education Secretary Michael Gove dismantled the London Challenge, favouring other improvement strategies such as Teach First, National Teaching Schools and relying on academies to drive up standards. In January 2013, Gove also announced that the National College and the Teacher Training Agency were to merge. It remains unclear whether the new agency – the National College for Teaching and Leadership – will pursue a vigorous collaboration agenda or whether schools, academy chains and other partnerships will be left free to make their own arrangements for support, challenge and ideas-sharing.

Whatever emerges once the dust has settled it is imperative that our best headteachers and leaders of the future play a prominent role in shaping these potentially seismic events. It is their vision, values and sense of what is best and right for children and young people that should determine the future of our school system rather than politically-driven initiatives or free-market ideology. It is hoped this book will focus debate on the great qualities our best headteachers possess – and why we should place our trust in them.

Appendix 1
The desert island challenge

Key qualities for headship as chosen by successful leaders.

Geoff Barton, Headteacher, King Edward VI High School, Bury St Edmunds, Suffolk

Here are my eight:

1 Vision.
2 Resilience.
3 Capacity to lead change.
4 Optimism.
5 Community leadership.
6 Development of staff.
7 Rigorous focus on raising standards.
8 Ability to innovate.

Llyn Codling, Executive Headteacher, Portswood and St Mary's Church of England primary schools, Southampton

These are the eight qualities that I believe you need to be a great leader. Ability to:

1 Listen.

2 Reflect.

3 Be decisive.

4 Not be afraid to make difficult decisions.

5 Meditate.

6 Control your own mind.

7 Be tenacious.

8 Serve.

Andrew Fleck, Headmaster, Sedbergh School, Cumbria

I have been Head of two schools for a total of nine years. From my first school I learned:

1 Prioritisation: there are limited resources in terms of time, money and skills – it is essential to deploy these efficiently and with clear priority. Prioritisation is painful because it disappoints people but it is essential in order to achieve outcomes.

2 Team-building: the sum of the parts is greater than the whole, more than that – it is how a shared vision is established. Without that vision, the school is inevitably diminished.

3 Empathy: we deal with thousands of people and empathy is essential to understand their situation and respond appropriately. By doing so, we defuse crises, build relationships, inspire achievement

and generate loyalty. It is the most important "soft skill" (but rarely assessed at interview).

4   Resilience – mental and physical: we have to respond to financial, educational and human issues. It *is* gruelling although I suspect the best heads make it so through their commitment and dedication. Despite that, burnout is a real risk and mental and physical strength is essential.

5   Determination: everywhere we turn there will be people who tell us that things cannot be done and conflicting demands. Headship has often been about achieving against the odds. That is through force of character and unwavering determination to see a project through to the end. (As an aside, I have seen a number of younger staff promoted to deputy head and headship, many of them have asked my advice prior to interviews. My starting point is to ask them what they would resign over – as deputy head or head one has to know the fundamental principles which one holds non-negotiable in order to be able to respond to unfamiliar situations and drive through difficult changes.)

6   Networking: it is not all determination that drives projects through to conclusion. Networking is team-building on a larger but looser scale. However it also opens up opportunities through chance meetings and conversations which grow to bigger things. It also enables us to gain an alternative vision and thereby circumvent or overcome obstacles.

So far, my second school has been about:

1   Giving people authority and autonomy in the knowledge that provided they try hard, I will back them up.

2   Challenging accepted wisdom.

3   Looking at small details.

4   Being visible – in Houses, classrooms and corridors.

5   The next challenge is to forge a longer-term vision to raise ten million pounds to invest in the fabric of the school.

Kenny Frederick, Principal, George Green's School, Tower Hamlets, London

1   Resilience is a key point for all headteachers – and this is
    something that can only be achieved in time, with experience, but
    also has something to do with your personality and way of thinking.
    For instance, I think heads need to be positive and optimistic and
    not be overwhelmed when things don't go to plan or when the
    government comes up with some new, seemingly impossible, target
    or initiative. Children and staff need someone who can help them
    see that the future is bright and that anything is possible.

2   Heads need to be able to communicate at all levels – with
    individuals as well as with the whole school. Much of my day
    is spent listening to staff and children and parents and trying
    to help them find a way of resolving their problems or at least
    acknowledging their pain and supporting them through it. This can
    weigh heavily on the mind!

3   Heads must always be calm – if you lose it what chance is there
    that everybody else can cope? However, this does not mean they
    have to be unemotional. You need to be able to feel for and express
    yourself to others (and indeed share your own pain with them). A
    cold unemotional fish just won't do it!

4   Heads must know their own strengths and weaknesses and
    acknowledge them to others. You should not try to appear perfect as
    you will get caught out. People appreciate honesty! Heads need to
    give honour to others and not claim every success as their own and
    every failure as somebody else's fault!

5   Heads need to appoint a team who complement each other and
    allow and enable people to grow and make mistakes without fear.

6   Heads need to respect others and not put others down – just because
    they can.

7   Heads need to remember nobody (especially them) is indispensible.
    The school can and will go on without you. A bit of humility goes a
    long way!

8 Heads need to develop others around them and demystify headship and encourage others to aim for the top job.

Richard Harman, Headmaster, Uppingham School, Rutland

The eight most important qualities that a 'great' headteacher should have:

1 Great instincts and judgement about people – recruiting the right staff and empowering them to do their jobs is the key to keeping your school moving forward.

2 Great vision – the ability to formulate and shape the future, rather than be shaped by 'events', allows you to see the wood for the trees.

3 Great opportunism – don't miss opportunities, as long as they fit within your overall vision: keep your wits about you and think tactically as well as strategically.

4 Great moral courage – know when to make a stand for what is right, even at the cost of short-term popularity. Remember you are a role model to many, adults as well as children.

5 Great optimism, resilience and energy – there are so many demands on your time and resources that you will need to do what it takes to keep yourself healthy and positive and keep taking the initiative when setbacks happen: resilience is a much under-rated quality.

6 Great communication skills – whether with pupils, staff, parents, press, alumni, visitors, the local community – you need to be able to deliver in writing and in person, set pieces and off-the-cuff talks alike.

7 Great wisdom – to know when to act quickly and when to reflect, when to 'nudge' and when to intervene, who to talk to and how to listen: something that only comes with experience.

8 Great commitment to the young – remember that it begins and ends with the best interests of those in your school, and more widely youngsters in all schools everywhere. It's all about them, not all about you.

And a cheeky number nine...

9 Great support – 'behind every great head' stands a team of great supportive people – family, friends, PA, deputy, senior management, governors/trustees. It may sometimes seem to others like a one-man show, but it certainly isn't – a great head is more like a great orchestral conductor than a great virtuoso performer.

Russell Hinton, Headteacher, The Brier School, Kingswinford, Dudley

Getting down to eight is hard and I may have cheated a little. In no particular order, but if I had to choose one it would be Number 4:

1 Knowledge of what you will be judged upon, i.e. Ofsted schedule, audit, local authority review.

2 Willingness to challenge accepted local thinking and beliefs; this will sometimes make you unpopular with potential future allies.

3 Readiness to respond quickly to immediate and unforeseen pressures.

4 Understanding that you are dealing with the most precious of things – people's children and all the hopes and dreams tied in with that.

5 Knowledge of strengths and weaknesses – your own, that of the staff and the organisation.

6 Acceptance that you cannot do everything yourself and you will need to delegate, but do check periodically.

7 Understand that this is a job that demands hard work and energy, but remains a job.

8 Acceptance that you will never finish the day with everything done and you are not indispensible.

Andrew Hutchinson, Executive Principal, Parkside Federation Academies, Cambridge

Top characteristics for me are:

1 Risk taker.

2 Rigorous attention to detail.

3 Empathy with school communities.

4 Selfless – organisation not ego.

5 Strong moral purpose.

6 Endurance.

Mike Kent, former Headteacher, Comber Grove Primary School, Camberwell, London

These are not in any particular order. Just thoughts…

1 To have a strong vision of what education is about, and for, and the determination to bring that vision about.

2 To be able to get the best out of people, not just someone who criticises their faults.

3 To be able to multi-task… calmly!

4 To recognise what constitutes a first class teacher.

5 To recognise, almost intuitively, which aspects of a school aren't working well.

6 To be sensitive, sympathetic and understanding towards people.

7 To have a wide range of outside interests.

8 To be efficient and practical in order to get things done.

9 To listen to everybody's view, but then to be decisive in action.

10 To be able to talk and communicate effectively to a range of audiences.

11 To have a good sense of humour.

12 To be able to cope effectively in a crisis.

13 To have a good knowledge of everything that's currently happening in education.

14 To be an excellent teacher, since the title is head*teacher.*

Dr John H Newton, Headmaster, Taunton School, Somerset

Eight qualities in no order at all:

1 Able to see things as they are not what the `school teachers' lens' suggests it is (Marcus Aurelius: `What is it, in itself?').

2 Patience with legislation, planning permission, logistics.

3 Able to see five years hence, and measure the present by the future when all around just see the present.

4 Heavenly minded AND of earthly use.

5 Slow to chide, swift to bless.

6 Love the sinner, hate the sin – in pupils, parents and staff.

7 Keep yourself intellectually fresh – and avoid being intellectually predictable.

8 Read a short novel's worth of info per day, assimilate it, and know what to do with it.

PS. I could think of lots more to do with being a CEO, with as much management speak as I can muster, but I think the job is more precious than that.

Catherine Paine, Executive Headteacher, Mount Street Academy and Saxilby Church of England Primary School, Lincolnshire

Here are my eight:

1   The ability to inspire others. The job is about winning hearts and minds: in the words of the late Steve Jobs, "To do great work and love what you do".

2   To be able to prioritise around relationships and results (not time and things).

3   To act as coach to your staff (and like all good sports coaches constantly urging: "Harder, faster, stronger").

4   To take the long term view and be able to say amidst complexity and confusion, "I know where this is going".

5   The ability to look like everything is under control (even when it isn't) and inspire confidence in others.

6   To step forward to take blame and step back when there is praise.

7   Faith (or something close to it) leading to deeply held values about human flourishing – which guide and shape every decision.

8   Tenacity – a dogged determination to never, never give up.

Hamid Patel, Principal and Chief Executive, Tauheedul Islam Girls' High School, Blackburn

An 'outstanding' leader in schools has the following qualities:

1   Visionary and optimistic: in the mundane, monotonous and highly-challenging environment of schools, it is important for staff to know where we are going – that today is better than yesterday and that tomorrow will be better than today.

2 Principled pragmatism: an outstanding leader is neither stuck in dogma that inhibits the ability of their organisation to respond to the needs and opportunities of the moment, nor so vested in self-interest and the 'whatever goes' mentality that they have no scruples, integrity or moral code. Instead, there is a third way: a way of principled pragmatism, where the principles inform but do not completely incarcerate the creativity of the organisation.

3 Foster moral intelligence not adherence: in their dealings with staff and students, outstanding leaders try not to use rewards and sanctions as a means of ensuring there is adherence to the rules and routines of the school. Instead, they invest heavily in creating a community that has a moral code it lives by, a moral covenant informed by the values and vision of the organisation – so that people choose to do the right thing because it is the right thing to do, not because there is a personal consequence for them.

4 Walk the walk: outstanding leaders have earned a clear moral authority to lead. People within the organisation are prepared to follow where the leader wants to lead. This is nourished through the leader having preparedness to expect of his or herself what they expect of everyone else – whether that is through their lesson planning, punctuality to meetings, smartness and interactions with colleagues and young people.

5 Self-managing and self-developing: outstanding leaders are prepared to recognise their faults and endeavour to change. They have excellent self-awareness and do not allow the trappings of their office or their authority to delude themselves about their capacities. If we are to inspire change in others, we must be prepared to change ourselves.

6 Listening and responsive: outstanding leaders invite dissent and are prepared to listen to the views of others. They distribute leadership of responsibilities and create ownership of a problem rather than hand out a list of tasks for their subjects to complete. They are prepared to listen to staff complaints and show that they are responsive to them. They also invite reasoned dissent from our young people, develop them to complain in a measured and constructive manner, and then show a willingness to respond to this.

The days of the absolute leader, who decided and does everything, has gone a long time ago.

7   Strategic: outstanding leaders have a strategic approach to managing their organisation. They do not let their immersion in the daily administrative grind of running the school prevent them from seeing the bigger picture. They are proactive in identifying and responding to opportunities and risks; energetic in their pursuit of excellence and have a zero tolerance of failure, waste and incompetence. They encourage responsible risk-taking and innovation by staff and learners; and they not just promote, but exemplify, the self-reflective and self-improving character needed to continuously progress.

8   Lucky: outstanding leaders (a bit like Napoleon's generals) are also lucky. They have excellent staff, highly competent and prepared to make the sacrifices needed. They have students who are focused and driven, who want to learn and achieve and who manage themselves. They are also leaders of the right school at the right time and find that their skills match the needs of the organisations and that their decisions stand the test of time.

9   Know the terrain: finally, outstanding leaders know their organisation in intimate detail. They know the strengths of the organisation and its people, its systems and its structures. They also know its limitations and weaknesses – not through a self-evaluation form, but because they feel the heartbeat of the organisation on a day-to-day level. They are also aware of what makes their organisation tick, the opportunities that they should exploit and the pitfalls that they need to avoid. As such, outstanding leaders make it their business to know their business.

Roger Pope, Principal, Kingsbridge Community College, Devon

1   Relationships: that comes first for me, and it is tied closely with values. Get the relationships right – open, trusting, humorous – and much else follows naturally. People feel motivated. They want

to follow you and want to do their best for you. It is tied with values because it is part of living what you are trying to model for students. It would be odd to be claiming to educate kids to be good citizens if you do not model those values in your everyday dealings with people. I also think work plays a big part in people's lives, and that a head therefore has a moral duty to make work as enjoyable and fulfilling as possible (I know of very successful heads who would put this much lower down their list because they work more through authoritative systems).

2   A culture of high expectations, relentless and restless searching for improvement. This has to run through at every level. People must not feel that nothing is ever good enough; they must always be wanting to move to the next level. It would be interesting to correlate really successful schools with the length of headship; I think it takes at least five or six years for the culture to embed and I suspect it is after that that interesting stuff really begins to happen.

3   Delegation and empowerment of staff: Call it distributed leadership if you will, but it's about trusting people to get on with the job so that they feel valued – and finding leadership opportunities for people from their NQT year onwards (I have just appointed my second NQT head of department).

4   Making things happen: You need constantly to inspire staff by making tangible things happen – new buildings, awards, perceivable gains in exam results.... They need to see concrete impact, not just talk, and they need to feel in the winners' corner.

5   Looking outwards: a lot has happened for us because I spend a lot of time doing stuff more widely – doing consultancy for the National College has brought me knowledge of other outstanding heads, made Teaching School possible and so on. You cannot take a school to new levels if you are insular.

Derek Pringle, Headmaster, St George's College, Quilmes, Buenos Aires, Argentina

The eight qualities which I'd take to my desert island (in no particular order of importance) are:

1 Being flexible, but with clear principles.

2 The capacity to listen *and* understand.

3 Thinking "out of the box".

4 Empowering staff.

5 Promoting teamwork.

6 Focused vision.

7 Not being afraid to say "no".

8 Knowing what is really happening in your school.

For me the most important is empowering staff, because a successful school can only exist with high quality motivated teachers.

Nigel Richardson, former Headteacher, The Perse School, Cambridge 1994–2008

1 Liking young people – and showing it: accept that the young will sometimes have harebrained views; expressing them in ways that get them into difficulties; that they will make mistakes in what they do – but never lose sight of the rewards of being able to help them make sense of life. If you meet them as prospective pupils, never concentrate only on their parents, ignoring them in the process.

2 Being reasonable, and explaining decisions – especially unpopular ones: teachers, parents, pupils and the wider public will all respond to it. Goodwill built up in good times makes people more likely to assume the best, rather than the worst, in bad times.

3 Making your assemblies challenging and interesting: they can be one of the most time-effective things you do; they set the tone. Within them, find original and inventive ways of emphasising regularly the importance of being kind, courteous and grateful to *all* members of the school community, regardless of their role or status – and practise what you preach.

4 Protecting the oddball, and encouraging the maverick pupil where possible: huge strides have been made to counter bullying, but the geek, the genius and the '12-year-old, going on 50' need more support. And schools have always been much better with convergent pupils than divergent ones. Conventional prefect systems spot one type of talent, but Young Enterprise often reveals leadership skills of a quite different order – and in some unexpected people.

5 Never forgetting the demands of teaching a nine-period day: nurture your staff; thank them regularly – and do all you can to improve their working conditions. Develop staff to the full, but also accept their limitations and all the other pressures on them.

6 Being balanced about the pros and cons of good administration: the value in MBWA (management by walking about) is very real. Too many of us get trapped inside our studies or offices, rather than being visible. That said, don't peddle the hoary old myth that efficient management systems are somehow only for faceless bureaucrats: they prevent duplication and waste of effort.

7 Being prepared to get the ablest governing body available and to get the best out of it: make full use of the skills-set you recruit. Don't look merely for the quiet life or the comfortable choices. Too much is written about the negative effects of governance: a good, questioning governing body can make a huge and beneficial difference.

8 Never losing the ability to laugh at oneself, or to admit mistakes: these are two of the most important abilities that all heads need, and too few have. Be confident. Use your prize-giving not *only* to congratulate yourself and your school but occasionally also to take a sideways look at your work and the nature of the job you do.

Lynn Slinger, Headteacher, Forest Way Special School, Leicestershire

My starter for eight is:

1 Vision.

2 Tenacity.

3 Stamina.

4 Positivity.

5 Charisma.

6 Drive.

7 Clarity.

8 Resilience.

Paul Smith, Principal, Parbold Douglas Church of England Academy, near Wigan, Lancashire

Eight things a great headteacher needs to turn a school around:

1 Perseverance: In the words of Jim Collins, "Few people attain great lives, in large part because it is just so easy to settle for a good life". The great headteacher has to have energy and perseverance. Impact change can happen when a new head comes to school. However, this change is not often sustained or embedded and it is after this initial impact that we need to have courage and perseverance to sustain the change that is needed. I once heard a speaker talk about "the long dark of the night" as Shakespeare's Henry V wrestles with his conscience about whether the action he has taken (battle of Agincourt) is correct or whether he should withdraw and change his plans. This is a decision many of us who have been faced with turning a school around have had to take. Are our decisions correct? What about the potential for conflict and loss ahead? As Shakespeare points out the night is often darkest before

the dawn. It is only through perseverance, courage and conviction that what we are doing is correct that we push through to the dawn and see the impact of the change as the school begins to improve in sometimes small and hard-to-define ways before the great leaps take place.

2   Talent spotting: not quite in the Simon Cowell model but it is important to have an analytical eye that tells you early on who will help you reach number one. A great leader needs a good team. It is important to beware the head-nodders who agree with anything you say; they often fail to deliver the goods. Give careful consideration to the ones who may seem most sceptical early on; they may be exactly the people you need most. A great leader cannot do it by themselves. Many would-be legendary generals have fallen alone at the front of the line turning to see that they didn't bother to bring the rest of the army with them. You need to quickly establish your team and begin to delegate responsibilities. One of the most important parts of being a team to me is having people who are incessantly optimistic but also willing to challenge poor performance at every turn.

3   Sense of humour: This helps to keep your own sanity and those around you! I also find it helps to keep a sense of perspective that can be easily lost when we find ourselves up to our ears in the trenches. A sense of humour helps to develop team spirit and get people on side with you even if at times it is a delirious or gallows humour. We have to remember that as headteacher we are responsible for setting the mood and the ethos for the school so the best headteachers can turn some of the most dire circumstances into positives or points for future development. It's amazing how a bit of blue sky thinking and talking can turn the gloomiest day around.

4   A plan: you need to have a plan for how to move school forward. The plan should start with an understanding of where the school is and how it got there. As a very famous sports coach often preaches, "If you don't know what you did, how do you know what to do?" A plan that can be shared and understood by all members of the school community is essential, with clear goals. As part of your plan it is important to spot quick wins. It is inevitable in a failing school that morale will be pretty low so those quick wins can turn

that around and get people ready for the long slog of truly turning the systems around that have got the school into the situation it is currently in.

5   Someone to talk to: we all need someone who will listen to our concerns and stories of incredulous behaviour and decision making. To fit in with this castaway theme we saw that Tom Hanks needed Wilson to be his person who he could tell everything to. The great leader on our desert island may need a Wilson or two!

6   To be a negotiator: during your time in turning around a school you are many things to many people. I have found myself crossing children over roads, putting grit on icy paths, mopping halls and even rescuing pets from trees. But the one thing I had to do on a daily basis was to negotiate. Negotiate with the local authority about the level of support needed and the level of time it will take to see things changing. Negotiate with governors, often around delicate manners. Negotiate with staff on changes to roles and responsibilities. Negotiate with parents about their role in school improvement.

7   See the bigger picture: the successful head must be able to see all the individual elements that make up a modern school and be able to marry them into a cohesive and successful organisation. They must be able to manage the conflicts between budgets and the need for extra resources and see that the office person is just as important in setting the tone for the school as the Year 6 class teacher.

8   Integrity and honesty: walk the walk as well as talk the talk. The great head has to be the vision. They have to balance being human and admitting fallibility against being wise. And they need to be someone people can rely on and trust.

Bernard Trafford, Headmaster, Royal Grammar School, Newcastle

1   Top comes Courage for me, because if you don't have that you can't keep on course and drive through the things that need doing when things get tough, nor to be open, consultative and approachable,

because asking people what they think doesn't always produce the answers or type of response you'd like. Determination is a subset of courage, as is confidence.

2   Vision (includes beliefs and principles).

3   Communication (i.e. the skills and the willingness, eagerness indeed, to get the message across).

4   Empathy (the ability and readiness to understand where others are coming from, why they find it hard to accept our vision and desire for change, how they suffer difficulties etc., includes tolerance too).

5   Patience (includes coping with the slowness with which things are sometimes achieved, taking the long view but also dealing with blocking and frustration). Determination is also a subset of patience.

6   Passion (without which you can't communicate the vision, find the commitment to and enthusiasm for putting the belief/principles into action).

7   Judgement (ability to pull all the pieces together, see the gaps and take action to bridge or plug them, make the organisation consistent and coherent etc.; also to make and justify tough decisions – see Courage).

8   Administration and finance (you must be able to do the sums, control finance, make the link between organisation/structure and cost).

Teresa Tunnadine, Headteacher, The Compton School, Finchley, London

I've given this some thought and the qualities are:

1   Clear moral purpose/vision necessary for raising standards.

2   Outstanding organisational skills – to know how to get things done in a logical sequential way.

3   Resilience – it will be tough and there will be a need to have tough conversations/make tough decisions for the greater good.

4   Confidence.

5   Determination.

6   Ability to find solutions/problem-solving approach combined with practical knowledge/experience.

7   Energy and positivity.

8   Excellent communication skills – oral and written: one-to-one and to large groups.

9   Emotional intelligence/humility and empathy.

Madeleine Vigar, Principal, The Castle Partnership Academy Trust, Haverhill, Suffolk

Eight key leadership qualities for school improvement:

1   Bravery.

2   Determination.

3   Humour.

4   Resilience.

5   Honesty/integrity.

6   Emotional intelligence.

7   Organisational, listening and communication skills – the ability to prioritise and manage time.

8   Ability to see "the wood and the trees".

Appendix 2
Attributes and professional characteristics

The list drawn up for the National Professional Qualification for Headship.

Professional characteristics shown by outstanding leaders:

- Optimistic, enthusiastic and curious – belief in people.
- Commitment to social justice, equity and excellence.
- Respect and empathy for others.
- Resilient – tireless energy.
- Persistent – in pursuit of excellence, putting pupils first.
- Drive and determination – ambitious.
- Courage, conviction and integrity.
- Vigilant and visible – "only the best will do".
- Humility plus professional will (fierce resolve).

Source: This list was compiled for a presentation on the NPQH by the National College for School Leadership in January 2011. It is based on the following research: *Outstanding Schools* series (Ofsted, 2009/10); *Capturing the Leadership Premium* (McKinsey 2010); Wisdom and Bus Schedules, Ron Glatter (*School Leadership and Management,* 2009); *The Future of Leadership,* S Crainer and D Dearlove (National College for School Leadership, 2008).

Appendix 3
Features of outstanding leadership

The leadership model at St John the Baptist School in Woking, Surrey.

Love This is at the heart of our work as leaders. Our role is to 'love' each person unconditionally and help them shine.

Example This means 'walking the talk' at all times. There is no middle ground! Crucially others need to trust you so that they will follow you. The examples you set or not will influence this!

Action Acting decisively ensures that others see your ability to deal with problems. The longer you leave it to act, the harder it becomes. Remember to preserve a person's dignity at all times.

Developing others Remember that 'without followers Napoleon was simply a man in a hat'. Providing opportunities for others to become more skilled is at the core of outstanding leadership. We cannot do it alone!

Effective communication Keep others informed so they feel empowered and valued. Listen to what others have to say and be visible, investing time in people as opposed to 'shuffling paper' or 'creating lists' in your office.

Reflection We are all on a learning journey. Through evaluating performance and continually seeking ways to improve, the journey of success is achievable.

Share your vision At SJB our vision is about ensuring students fulfil their potential. It is important that you explain what this means to your teams and explain the benefits of achieving this aim.

Humility Never use your power or title when dealing with others. A leader should 'support, challenge and inspire' others for the benefit of all.

Integrity Integrity means 'doing the right thing when no one is looking'. It means never asking anyone to do something you would not be prepared to do yourself. It is our golden rule of strong leadership.

Positivity Aim to be positive at all times, promoting a 'can-do attitude'. Manage your emotions upwards to ensure negativity is kept to a minimum. Remember we have chosen to be here. So enjoy it!

This leadership model is reproduced by kind permission of Ani Magill, Headteacher of St John the Baptist School.

Bibliography

Capturing the Leadership Premium, by Sir Michael Barber, Fenton Whelan and Michael Clark (McKinsey 2010).

Creating Learning without Limits by Mandy Swann, Alison Peacock, Susan Hart and Mary Jane Drummond (Open University Press, 2012).

Emotional Intelligence: Why it can matter more than IQ by Daniel Goleman (Bantam, 1995).

Good to Great: Why some companies make the leap... and others don't by Jim Collins (Random House, 2001).

How Successful Headteachers Survive and Thrive by Professor Tim Brighouse (RM, 2007).

Rethinking Educational Leadership: From improvement to transformation by Professor John West-Burnham (Continuum 2009).

The Future of Leadership by S Crainer and D Dearlove (National College for School Leadership, 2008).

'The Uppingham Revolt: Public school pupils say they were RIGHT to stage mass mutiny over expelled schoolmates' by Neil Sears and Rebecca Camber, *Daily Mail* 5th May 2010.

System Leadership through Extended Headship Roles: Research associate full report by Teresa Tunnadine (National College for School Leadership, Spring 2011).

Twelve Outstanding Secondary Schools: Excelling against the odds (Ofsted, 2009).

Twenty Outstanding Primary Schools: Excelling against the odds (Ofsted, 2009).

What Makes a Great School? by Andy Buck (National College for School Leadership and the City Challenge Programme, 2009).

'What Makes a Leader?' By Daniel Goleman (Harvard Business Review, 1998).

'Wisdom and Bus Schedules: Developing school leadership' by Ron Glatter (*School Leadership and Management*, 29(3) pp. 225–237, 2009)..

50 Great Things Leaders Do: Let's get fired up! by Dr Frank Rudnesky (lulu.com 2011).

Further reading

Tweak to Transform: Improving teaching: a practical handbook for school leaders by Mike Hughes with David Potter (Network Continuum Education, 2002).

Understanding Systems Leadership: Securing excellence and equity in education by Professor Dame Pat Collarbone, co-authored with Professor John West-Burnham (Network Continuum Education, 2008).

Nudge: Improving decisions about health, wealth and happiness by Richard H Thaler and Cass R Sunstein (Penguin, 2009).

Tales from the Head is Room: Life in a London primary school by Mike Kent (Continuum, 2001).

Index